Isabella Burt

Historical Notices of Chelsea, Kensington, Fulham, and Hammersmith

With Some Particulars of Old Families

Isabella Burt

Historical Notices of Chelsea, Kensington, Fulham, and Hammersmith
With Some Particulars of Old Families

ISBN/EAN: 9783337186807

Printed in Europe, USA, Canada, Australia, Japan

Cover: Foto ©ninafisch / pixelio.de

More available books at **www.hansebooks.com**

HOLLAND HOUSE, KENSINGTON

Historical Notices of Chelsea, Kensington, Fulham, and Hammersmith.

WITH

SOME PARTICULARS OF OLD FAMILIES.

ALSO

An Account of their Antiquities and Present State.

BY

ISABELLA BURT,

AUTHORESS OF "THE LORD'S PRAYER FAMILIARLY EXPLAINED,"
"MEMORIALS OF THE OAK TREE," ETC. ETC.

J. SAUNDERS,
22, HIGH STREET, KENSINGTON.
1871.

DRYDEN PRESS.
J. DAVY AND SONS, 137, LONG ACRE, LONDON.

THE MOST NOBLE
THE MARCHIONESS OF THOMOND.

MADAM,

     With your kind permission, I herewith dedicate the following pages to your Ladyship, with the wish that they were more worthy of the honour of your patronage.

I take this opportunity of recording my gratitude for all your goodness to me, and have the honour to be,

        MADAM,

      Your Ladyship's most humble,

          Very grateful servant,

            ISABELLA BURT.

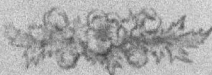

CONTENTS.

PARISH OF KENSINGTON

PARISH OF FULHAM.

PARISH OF HAMMERSMITH.

Historical Notices

OF

CHELSEA, KENSINGTON, FULHAM, AND HAMMERSMITH.

INTRODUCTION.

THE four large Parishes about to be described present important claims to our notice. It is true that nearly all the green fields, and nearly all the fine old trees, once so numerous in them, have been ravaged and cut down by that large army who wield the hod and mortar. They are now no longer sweet pretty villages for a summer day's excursion, although many "fine views," pretty walks, and nooks may be found by the curious pedestrian, more especially in FULHAM, which still retains a good deal of its rurality; while CHELSEA has its Cheyne Walk, and the grounds of the Royal Hospital; HAMMERSMITH its Malls, upper and lower, and KENSINGTON offers its stately

CHELSEA PARISH CHURCH.

Parish of Chelsea.

CHAPTER I.

OF the four Parishes now under consideration, perhaps CHELSEA offers the strongest claims to our notice; for among the suburban resorts of our holiday excursionists, there are none that are more suggestive of historical reminiscences of the most interesting character. True it now can boast no rural recommendations by way of "walks" and "groves of trees," for multitudes of middling sized houses have encroached upon, and spread over the greater part of it, covering each green field and meadow so that the pedestrian is lost in a wilderness of "streets" and "rows" of the most uninteresting description. These have completely disguised nearly all the spots so well known to history, and so dear to that class who love to ascertain ancient localities. More especially the old abiding places of those who in the exciting periods of the "olden time" played a conspicuous part for good or ill; and left, as the case might be, a dishonoured or ennobled name to their posterity.

But if Chelsea is wanting in the natural beauties it was once so admired for, it has acquired other recommendations, and objects of interest which attract numerous visitors. In no place above London Bridge does the Thames spread its gently flowing waters into so noble an expanse as it does here; where it is known as the "Reach," and which extending two miles east and west, exhibits, when the tide is at the full, a truly noble sight, and also affords ample means for all kinds of aquatic amusements. The Royal Hospital for old soldiers, with its extensive and handsome gardens; the Royal Military Asylum for their children; that eminent Institution St. Mark's College and Training School; the fine old Parish Church, containing so many beautiful monuments; and the new elegant Church of St. Luke's, not forgetting Cremorne Gardens and the Botannical Gardens, are all attractions for the holiday visitors who never fail in the summer to ramble over this old parish.

Few persons are aware that some really fine views may be obtained from the upper windows of the old houses in Chelsea; more particularly from those standing in CHEYNE ROW, a place that still bears evidences of its former wealthy and aristocratic residents. Indeed, the antiquities of Chelsea are chiefly by the water side. A walk of about three quarters of a mile from Manor Street to Cremorne Gardens presents nearly all the existing antiquities now to be found in Chelsea.

Not wishing to trouble the reader with long anti-quarian details, it may suffice to briefly explain the derivation of the name of *Chelsea*. The earliest records of this old parish are to be found in the Saxon Chronicle of 785, where it is mentioned that a Synod was held here during the residence of Offa King of the Mercians, who in that year met in solemn council various bishops and archbishops. But, as historians, in one respect at least, resemble doctors, and do not always agree, various etymologies have been assigned to it. The most reliable authorities, however, consider it to be derived from the Saxon word *Ceale-hythe*, or *a landing place for chalk*, this part of the river, in the then inefficient state of land carriage, being the most convenient place for landing a substance not found in the soil of Chelsea, or contiguous districts. After the Norman invasion, the Norman-French name of *Chaussee* was bestowed on it, from the circumstance of finding some strong and ancient embankments along the water side. They are attributed to the Romans, and are at this time apparently as good as ever, and whether made by the Romans or not, have for ages sufficed to keep the Thames from overflowing its banks at this part of its course. *Chaussee* signifies *causeway*. The amalgamation of Ceale-hythe and Chaussee has gradually produced the word Chelsea, which name it has borne for about three hundred years

Chelsea must have been a very agreeable place for a long period of its history. Situated on ground gradually rising to about fifteen feet above the water level, and laid out with the parks and grounds of the nobility and gentry, and interspersed with beautiful nursery grounds, fine meadows and noble trees, no wonder that for about three centuries it was the dwelling place of all the celebrities of those ages: of all the fashionable and aristocratic. Although so near London, it does not

lie in the London chalk basin. Its geological for-
mation is first a rich dark soil which has for ages
been highly dressed, owing to the successive residence of rich landed proprietors of extensive grounds
and gardens, and also as having for a long period so
many large nursery grounds. For years all kinds of
known flowers and plants were here brought as
nearly as possible to perfection ; to do so, the soil
has been so richly dressed as to be even now very
productive. This soil lies on a bed of siliceous
gravel about five feet thick, lying on a strata of stiff
blue clay several hundred feet in depth ; beneath
this a marine deposit of shells, &c., showing that
like many other places it must at some remote age
have been covered by the sea. The air of Chelsea is
mild, and good for consumptive and asthmatic complaints, but it is not bracing, and in the autumn it
is very debilitating ; while in certain situations, and
at particular seasons, it is subject to very keen cold
winds.

Chelsea is bounded on its south by the noble
" Reach," on the north the Fulham Road divides it
from Kensington, on the east lies St. George's and
Hanover Square. Two small rivulets, now arched
over, formerly ran through green meadows, and
divided it on the east and west from St. George's
and Fulham. The Parish of Chelsea is about one
mile and a half long, by about a mile and a quarter
broad. Its area numbers 865 statute acres. In the
census of 1801 it was found to contain 11,604
inhabitants. In 1861 the population had increased
to 63,439.

CHAPTER II.

CHELSEA PARISH CHURCH is conspicuously placed near the "Reach." It is very ancient; no thoughtful person can look on its venerable exterior without emotions of reverence and interest. Time has dealt gently with it, and mellowed its surface into an agreeable tint. It is principally built of brick, the north and south chapels are of stone; it consists of a nave, two chancels and two aisles. The most ancient part of it was built in the reign of Edward II., when the district was constituted into a Rectory, Roger D. Berners being its first Rector, while the King was the Patron. It has a noble tower, built in 1668, and at that time was believed to be (as probably it was) the highest piece of brickwork in England. It is one hundred and thirty feet high and twenty-four feet wide.

As the church had fallen into decay it underwent a thorough renovation. The old parts were restored, the inside paved, and the churchyard enclosed, while Lady Jane Cheyne was at the sole charge of a new roof. It possesses six good bells, and also another bell, "the Ashburnham bell," given to it under very peculiar circumstances. In the year

1679, the Honourable William Ashburnham, one foggy evening missed his footing, and got into the river, and would no doubt have been drowned, but that the old church clock striking the hour of nine guided him to land and safety. In gratitude for this narrow escape he presented the church with a new bell. The churchwardens with good taste have placed this pious memento of an interesting event just inside the ancient porch, with a suitable inscription.

The church has a good clock; on the outside of the tower is a sun dial. Lower down on the wall is a large handsome tablet to the memory of the learned Dr. Chamberlayne. Three of his sons and his daughter lie in a vault near. The latter was too remarkable a character to be passed over. Born with amazonian tastes she naturally acquired mascu line habits, and was of a bold and noble disposition. Nature indeed made a mistake in enfolding so martial a spirit in a female form. However, she played a man's part, for she assumed the dress of a man, and went to sea in a fire-ship in June 1690 under her brother's command, and fought the French in an action of six hours with the most undaunted bravery. The epitaph on her tomb names her as a second "Pallas, chaste and fearless," and that sudden death called her away, leaving no projeny like herself "worthy to rule the main." She was married at the conclusion of her adventures to a John Spragg, Esq. A newspaper of 1692 records these circumstances, and the *Gazetteer* newspaper of

October 30, 1788, reprinted it. These papers also mention that another English *lady* was serving as a volunteer in the French army in Piedmont.

In the south east corner of the churchyard, very near the water, is a beautiful monument to the memory of Sir Hans Sloane and his lady, composed of Portland stone. On the top, under a portico, supported by four pillars, is placed a vase of pure white marble, with four serpents beautifully executed, out of one piece, and done by a Mr. Wilton a statuary. The arms, the crest, and two inscriptions are on the four sides.

Near to this is a handsome obelisk to Phillip Miller, author of the "Gardener's Dictionary," and sometime curator of the Botanical Gardens at Chelsea. In another part of the churchyard is a flat stone recording that Woodfall, the printer of "*Junius' Letters*" lies there.

Besides these, the churchyard, and the outside walls are filled and nearly covered with various stones and tablets to the memory of the numerous wealthy inhabitants of Chelsea. The interior is also crowded with all sorts of tombs, tablets, and monuments, which bear testimony to the wealth and position of the former residents of this old parish.

Amongst the most curious is a handsome monument to Sir John Stanley, composed of different coloured marbles, two figures, life size, of Justice and Fortitude, support a tablet, on which is placed one of the most fulsome epitaphs ever penned in memory of the dead. It is well composed, but too long to quote ; its chief point is, that to say a *Stanley* lies here, is epitaph enough, and that nothing

> "Can dignify his grave, or set it forth
> Like the immortal fame of his own worth!"

Another to two of his children is very pretty.

> "The Eagle death found where the infants lay,
> And in his talons bore their souls to Heaven.
> Let no profane hand these reliques sever,
> But as they lye, so let them rest for ever."

There is a large and ancient altar tomb to the memory of the Brays, a noble family of knights, of whom many members were here buried. Age has defaced, and time obliterated, all but those simple and beautiful words so often seen on old tombs. "*Of your charitie pray for the soul of Edmund Lord Bray.*" No inscription however long or well written can convey a deeper sense of *penitent humble* piety than is intimated in these quaint lines—so brief, and yet so forcible.

Against the south wall of the upper chancel is placed a large upright flat tomb to the memory of the celebrated Sir Thomas More. It is plain but rich : under a gothic arch is a large slab of black marble with a long Latin inscription written by himself. Both this and the tomb were placed there during his life, with a blank left for dates. Sir Thomas More was born in Milk Street, London. He married twice, and had three daughters and one son. He built himself a large handsome mansion in extensive grounds adjoining the Church. The description of his life, piety, and gentleness during his long residence as set forth by various biographers is very edifying: but no true member of the enlightened faith will quite forgive his furious and cruel zeal in persecuting *heretics*.

Sir Thomas was a constant attendant at divine service at Chelsea Church, frequently assisting in the celebration of the mass; one of the small chapels was built by him and is still called by his name. He was also very charitable. It is a tradition of the place that he hired a house to entertain old and distressed persons in; his beloved and favourite daughter Margaret had it in charge to see that they wanted nothing. Although Sir Thomas's tomb is in Chelsea Church, it has been a matter of dispute, not yet settled, whether or no his body was buried there, or in London. His head, however, was obtained by his daughter Margaret Roper, who enclosed it in a silver casket, for which she was imprisoned. It was buried with her.

On the south wall is the large and elegant monument of Jane Duchess of Northumberland. To the right of her tomb are the effigies of the Duchess and her five daughters all kneeling, and very gracefully executed. The whole is under a gothic canopy, supported by mosaic pillars, which together with the tomb is richly ornamented. The figure of the Duchess is also richly ornamented in enamel, representing her in the full dress of her order.

On the same wall is a magnificent and beautiful monument to the memory of Gregory Lord Dacre, and Ann his wife. They are represented in white marble lying side by side, with a dog at their feet.

The whole tomb, which forms a gothic canopy, is very richly ornamented with flowers beautifully done, and several elaborate pieces of mosaic work.

Another beautiful monument and effigy of Lady Jane Cheyne was the work of the celebrated Bernini, and cost £500. The effigy of the Lady is in white marble as large as life, reclining on a black marble sarcophagus, under an arch of veined marble supported by elegant pillars of the Corinthian order; the figure is slightly raised, with one hand on the Bible. Remarkable in life for her goodness and charity, she was a munificent benefactor to Chelsea. She came of a noble stock, being a daughter of the Duke of Newcastle, and married Charles Cheyne, Esq., Lord of the Manor, and died in 1669.

The Lawrence Chapel is also interesting; it contains several good monuments to the Lawrence family, who lived for many generations in Chelsea. The handsomest of these is one to Thomas Lawrence, Esq., with a quaint epitaph :—

> " The years wherein I lived was fifty-fowre,
>   October twenty-eight did end my life ;
> Children five of eleven God left in store,
>   To be comfort of thayre mother and my wife ;
> The world can say what I have been before,
>   What I am now examples still are rife.
> Thus Thomas Lawrence speaks to tymes ensving,
> That death is sure, and Tyme is past reneving."

Near to this last, is a very old monument to Thomas Hungerford, Esq., in carved stone, with effigies of himself, wife, and nine sons and daughters;

all kneeling, according to their ages, in the quaint stiff dress of the times. He seems to have played a conspicuous part from the reign of Henry VIII. to Queen Elizabeth, having been the faithful servant of four monarchs in various capacities, displaying in each no small amount of ability and tact.

Another small, but elegant white marble monument to the memory of two sisters, is much admired. It consists of two marble urns under a portico.

Not wishing to tire the reader, only the most beautiful of the monuments have been noticed; although they all merit attention. Indeed, very few churches contain so many remarkable tombs and tablets as this ancient edifice. Numbers of persons who take interest in such things come a long way for no other reason than to see them, take drawings, &c.

The interior is so decorated, so venerable and time-worn, that one wonders how a ponderous dark wooden gallery, placed at the west end, was allowed to disfigure it. In addition to it, there are pews nearly breast high to match; these are not ornamented, and are in the most common-place style. Nothing can be more out of keeping with the beautiful pieces of antiquity in the church, than these. On the south wall hangs a memento of monkish times. A Bible, Prayer Book, Church Homilies, and Fox's Book of Martyrs, are all chained over a mahogany shelf. The altar-piece is very plain. The font is modern. The pulpit is of oak, ornamented with foliage.

Some of the Churchwardens' accounts are amusing :—

    1668. Paid the Parish for Prayer Book for
        the Prince of Wales £0 1 0
    1699. Paid the ringers the day the King
        went over the ferry 1 0 0

The ringers were also paid for some warlike services we scarcely think they performed: —

    1706. Paid the ringers for taking Madrid . £0 10 0
    1708. Paid the ringers for taking Lisle . 0 10 0
    1179. Paid the ringers for taking the Citadel
        of Tourney 0 10 0

The Parish Register, part of it written in a beautiful handwriting, commences in the year 1559. Among the remarkable events connected with the church may be mentioned that, owing to some unusually high spring tides in 1809, the Thames flowed quite up to the old walls, and many persons who chose to go under such circumstances, were rowed in a boat to church.

CHAPTER III.

THE ROYAL HOSPITAL for old and disabled soldiers is surely one of the noblest results of well-directed benevolence we have in the country. It stands on the site of a college founded in the reign of James I. as a training college for divines, in which to be exercised in various controversial themes. But, after undergoing various discouragements and difficulties, it failed. It was called King James' College.

The Royal Hospital is in the King's Road. The building is quiet, but imposing. Its gardens, which were originally laid out in an ugly form, with two small, absurd canals, are now arranged according to the modern notions respecting these things. Its canals have been filled in, and laid over with grass plats, gravel walks, and flower-beds. In the winter these gardens are sheltered from the winds; while in the summer they are very pleasant, and much admired and enjoyed by the neighbouring inhabitants and sight-seers. All the charming views once to be seen over the river are of course blocked out by the numberless erections at all points, which have sprung up of late years.

The well-known tradition that the erring, but

amiable Nell Gwynne, was the original projector of
this place, seems to have a good foundation. One
or two newspapers of the time noticed the circumstance, while an anonymous writer of her life states it
as a fact—namely, that one day, when she was riding
in her coach, a man who was, or pretended to be an
old soldier returned from the wars at Tangiers,
begged charity of her. Affected to tears, she took
the first opportunity of intreating the King to pa-
tronise any scheme that might be suggested to
provide for the support of wounded, aged and sick
soldiers—persons who had spent their lives and
shed their blood for their country. She also interested many noble and influential persons in this
cause ; among them Sir Stephen Fox, ancestor of
the Lords Holland. He was one of the most liberal
and zealous of its founders. Chelsea Hospital was
built from designs of Sir Christopher Wren ; it was
begun in 1682, and finished in 1690, at the cost of
£150,000. Charles II. laid the first stone. The
Hospital, with its gardens, principal buildings, courts
and offices, all attached, occupy about fifty-four square
acres. It has three large courts or squares. It is
built of red brick, toned down by time and weather.
It is a sober, imposing looking edifice, and adapted
with good taste in every respect for the comfort and
recreation of worn-out veterans.

The most stately entrance is from the King's
Road, through an avenue of trees to the Queen's
Road, where admission is gained through some high
and handsome gates. They open into a spacious
and lofty vestibule. Steps to the right and left

conduct to the dining hall on one side, and the
chapel on the other. These are both one hundred
and ten feet long. The dining hall is not now used
for meals, but is furnished with some books, and
used as a lounging and smoking room. At one end
is a very large picture of Charles II., with allegorical figures, the face of Nell Gwynne being introduced at the corner. It was painted by Norris, and
is beautifully done. At the other end, in centre of
the gallery, are the Royal arms, elegantly carved on
an oaken shield. Over the gallery is (or will be
very shortly) another fine picture of the Duke of
Wellington in a triumphal car, trampling on the
emblems of War and Rebellion; while Victory is
crowning him. Peace is following with her train.
This is painted by Ward.

The Chapel is paved with black and white
marble, and the wainscot is of Dutch oak. It was
consecrated by Compton, Bishop of London. The
Bishop of London and the Rector of Chelsea have
certain rights and immunities connected with the
Hospital, which were duly arranged at the time of
consecration, and are very stringent. The chapel
has an altar piece representing the Sepulchre watched
by Roman soldiers. It was painted by Sebastian
Ricci.

The altar is also elegantly decorated with carvings
by Grinling Gibbons. The roofs of both hall and
chapel are hung with a variety of flags both old and
new, and standards taken in the various battles.
The vestibule conducts to a handsome large square.
In the centre of this stands a bronze statue of

Charles II., dressed in a *Roman habit*. Why are
Englishmen so often pourtrayed in this garb?
What similarity is there between sturdy John Bull
and an ancient Roman? It is so out of keeping,
and disturbs one's notions of the fitness of things.

The square opens to the south, overlooking the
gardens. On the side that joins the building runs
an elegant colonnade, which is useful in winter and
a shelter from the heat in summer.

East and west of this square are two long ranges
of buildings, in which the greater part of the old
soldiers are lodged. On the other side of these
buildings are two large courts. At this time, De-
cember 1870, there are 537 pensioners.

The private soldiers are well fed, comfortably
lodged, and warmly clothed, and receive seven pence
a week and one pint of beer daily.

A Cemetery is attached to the Hospital. The
first old soldier buried there was Simon Bax, and
he must have had an eventful life, and at all events
performed his duty to his country; for he had
served in the army during four reigns—Charles I.,
Charles II., James II., and lastly William III. The
remains of many brave officers lie there. And
in 1739 a Mrs. Christian Davis, known as "Mother
Ross," was interred with military honours, she having
in man's attire served well and bravely as a soldier
in some of the campaigns under King William and
the Duke of Marlborough. Hannah Snell, another
female soldier, was buried in this place. She en-
listed in a regiment of foot in 1744. After serving
in it for some years, she deserted, and joined the

Marines. Being severely wounded, she was sent to England, and rewarded for her bravery with a pension of £30. a year. She also had a pension from the Hospital, and always wore her uniform.

There is an amusing epitaph to one William Hiselend, stating that at *one hundred* years of age he *married*. One wonders how old his bride was, or whether, like him, she was in second childhood. He had served in the army eighty years. At his death in 1732 he was one hundred and twelve years old.

The once famous and elegant RANELAGH GARDENS, which, with the Earl of Ranelagh's House, adjoined the Hospital, are now Crown property, and have been assigned for the recreation of the inhabitants of the Hospital. The public are admitted, with certain restrictions. These gardens were once very famous, and the resort of the nobility and gentry, who were attracted by the singing and dancing. It was conducted with the utmost propriety and elegance, to suit its aristocratic visitors. It was furnished with a pretty Rotunda. The company promenaded round at their pleasure.

An excellent School for the daughters of old soldiers is attached to the Hospital. It was founded and endowed by Lady Elizabeth Hastings and some others, whom she had interested in her benevolent plan. She was the daughter of the Earl of Huntingdon, and was born 1682, dying in 1739. In the forty-second number of the "Tatler," her character and life is fully described by Sir Richard Steele, under the name of Aspasia.

CHAPTER IV.

HE ROYAL MILITARY ASYLUM, or, as popularly called, the " Duke of York's School" for the children of soldiers of the regular army, is situated near the Hospital. It stands on the site of a handsome house which belonged to the Cadogan family. It was purchased and pulled down to make way for this fine institution. The foundation stone was laid by the Duke of York in June, 1801, accompanied by a large number of general officers and a great many of the nobility. The sound principles of policy and humanity which originated this establishment, and which are still exercised in carrying it on, are an honour to an enlightened age, and congenial to our benevolence. It provides for so many helpless numbers of the community in such a practical, sensible way, that this asylum is justly held in great estimation. Here children of both sexes are clothed, well and amply fed, comfortably lodged and decently educated, and grounded in the principles of Christianity.

The building is spacious and handsome, built of brick, and formed into three sides of a quadrangle. It has an elegant stone balustrade in front, with a fine portico, also of stone. It consists of four large columns supporting a pediment, with frieze running round, the Royal arms in the centre. It has two large dining-rooms and two large stone rooms, in which the boys, every morning, winter and summer, are plunged into cold baths.

Near these rooms are two large school-rooms, in which they learn to read and write and cast accounts. They are also drilled, and undergo a military training, and are indeed soldiers in miniature. They excite a good deal of attention and interest whenever they are taken into public places; and indeed it would be difficult to find a finer body of sturdy, healthy boys, than these. London has few pleasanter sights to show than these embryo soldiers marching along with their band, which is played with considerable ability, considering the youth of the performers.

The large piece of ground in front is laid out in a handsome way, planted with trees, and ornamented with grass-plats and flower-beds, with gravel walks and seats. The Duke of York, by whose instrumentality the asylum was established, took much pride and pleasure in the result of his exertions. He constantly visited it, and was always interested in its welfare, taking much notice of the boys. At his last visit, he was affected to tears by their crowding round and cheering him. "God bless you, my lads," he said. And departing, they saw their benefactor no more.

There are some excellent schools of various kinds in Chelsea. Of these, the parochial schools are large and flourishing. The building for them is particularly neat and commodious. The Hon. and Rev. J. Wellesley laid the first stone in June, 1324.

The WHITELAND TRAINING INSTITUTION, in the King's Road, is well known and duly appreciated. It provides for the education and maintenance of more than one hundred young women between the ages of eighteen and twenty-five. Here they are trained with a view of becoming skilled teachers in the National Schools, and also as daily teachers in four schools in the neighbourhood. It is patronised by Miss Burdett Coutts and other ladies of consideration. The premises are extensive. An old house is attached, which for a long series of years has been used for educational purposes.

ST. MARK'S COLLEGE is an institution on similar principles, for training young men as schoolmasters, in connexion with the Established Church. It is divided into the Upper, Middle, and Lower Schools. The first gives a superior education to boys, including Latin and French. The Lower is for the humbler classes. The premises are very extensive. The grounds alone, which are laid out partly as flower gardens, partly as playgrounds, occupy eleven acres.

The old house assigned as the residence of the principal is one of the old Chelsea houses, with a history attached to it. In the reign of Elizabeth, Stanley House formed part of the estate of Sir Arthur Gorges. He was the friend of Spenser the poet, who wrote a beautiful elegy on Lady Gorges, entitled the "Daphniad." The house, after being occupied by a variety of residents, became in 1777

the property of that unhappy Countess of Strath-
mere who married the infamous A. Bowes, Esq.
Her ladyship was one of the best female botanists
of the age. She built large greenhouses and extensive hothouses, filling them with rare and beautiful
exotics. Her wretched husband, as a part of his
systematic cruelty to her, destroyed them.

Jesse Foot, in his " Life of Bowes," has given a
shocking account of his barbarities to her. At
length, however, she got a separation, under heavy
securities. Worn out in body and mind, the poor
lady died in 1800. He met with his deserts, and
died miserably in jail.

St. Mark's College was established by the National Society, who bought this old house and fitted
it for the residence of the head master or principal.
The buildings forming the schools are in the Italian
style, with a neat chapel, containing windows of
stained glass. A large number of boys are educated
here. Also one hundred young men are trained as
schoolmasters. Indeed, this institution is one of the
most eminent of its kind in this country.

The SCHOOL OF DISCIPLINE is the oldest Reformatory for young girls in London or the suburbs.
It was opened by the famous Mrs. Elizabeth Fry.
It was established in Chelsea in 1825. It is a
certified Industrial School, reforming, boarding,
clothing and educating begging, homeless girls.
They are paid for by the Home Office.

CHAPTER V.

WHEN designated the "VILLAGE OF PALACES," Chelsea must have been an elegant place, and at all events was a highly favourite one. A mere list of those who lived here is suggestive of the most stirring events in history, and brings to mind the actions and characters of those celebrated individuals who have left so many impressions of themselves in the literary productions and works of art of their times, and who were distinguished as warriors, statesmen, painters, or poets.

The first nobleman mentioned as living at Chelsea was the celebrated warrior the Earl of Warwick, renowned for his prowess at the battles of Cressy and Poictiers. His house has long since gone. His successors in the residence were first the Bishop of Salisbury, and afterwards it was granted by Richard III. to the widowed Duchess of Norfolk for her life, to be held by the elegant service of a red rose. The Marquis of Berkeley also lived there. He was an adherent of Henry VII.

George Earl of Shrewsbury, who had the custody of Mary Queen of Scots, lived for some time at Chelsea, leaving his residence there to his wife,

Elizabeth, one of the most beautiful women of that time, and remarkable for her extraordinary good fortune in marriage. Having had successively four husbands all wealthy or noble, she lived as a widow for seventeen years, and from her position, great wealth and rank, excercised considerable power. She built three noble mansions, Chatsworth, Old-cotes, and Hardwicke.

In this parish, as well as the other three treated of in this work, numbers of old houses rendered interesting by remarkable residents, have been destroyed.

The most interesting of these, the mansion built for himself by the celebrated Sir F. Thomas More, Lord High Chancellor in the reign of Henry VIII., and who lost his head by his obstinacy in denying the King's supremacy, has long since disappeared. He went to Chelsea about 1520, his house and grounds, which adjoined the Church, were, as Erasmus describes them, " Neither mean nor subject to envy," yet magnificent and commodious.

Beaufort Street and Row, and other houses, have been erected on the spot. Parts of the very high walls which bounded his grounds are left in many places, and confine the gardens belonging to the houses in Beaufort Street.

The porter's lodge not many years since was an interesting and picturesque relic. It was the well known " Clock House." A builder who purchased it found the interior so very inconvenient, that he (although with regret) pulled it down, erecting a more convenient place. The old garden, or at least what is left of it, is shewn. A very aged twisted mulberry tree is pointed out as having in its day supplied Queen Elizabeth with many a plate of its fruit; also the gate (although blocked up) is shewn through which Sir Thomas passed on his way to the boat that conveyed him to the Tower.

After the attainder and death of Sir Thomas More, the house became the residence of the Marquis of Winchester, Lord High Treasurer in the reign of Queen Elizabeth; Lord Dacre succeeded. His widow, who only lived a few months after his death, left the house to her brother, the great Lord Burleigh. At his lordship's death it fell to his younger son the Earl of Salisbury, who sold it to the half mad Earl of Lincoln. He was one of the peers who sat on the trial of Mary Queen of Scots, and also on the trial of the Earl of Essex. His lordship's descendant Sir Henry Gorges, who also lived here, left some curious memoirs of his life and exploits.

Cranfield, Earl of Middlesex, Lord High Trea- surer, was the next possessor. Commencing as merchant of the city of London; he gradually rose from one high post to another only to have a great fall. For offending his patron, the Duke of Buck- ingham, his treasurer's staff was taken from him, and he became imprisoned in the Tower, while the Duke coolly took possession of his house at Chel- sea in 1626. This was the celebrated Duke of Buckingham, the favourite and friend of James the First, and who was assassinated at Portsmouth by Felton in 1628. The house, which had previously undergone many alterations, was then called

BUCKINGHAM HOUSE. His lordship's daughter, the Duchess of Lennox, resided in it. Passing from her into various tenancies, it became the residence of the second Duke of Buckingham, who, after a profligate life, died very poor, leaving none to lament him.

The Marquis of Bristol was its next tenant. It was afterwards sold to the Duke of Beaufort; various members of this noble family occupied it until the year 1720. The house, on coming into the possession of the Beaufort family, was called BEAUFORT HOUSE. In 1738 it was purchased by the celebrated Sir Hans Sloane. Eventually it was pulled down in 1740. The gate, which was built by Inigo Jones, was given by Sir Hans Sloane to the Earl of Burlington, who placed it in his grounds at Chiswick.

While Sir Thomas More lived in this remarkable house he received many guests, whose names are of historical interest. Hans Holbein the painter resided with him for three years. Erasmus the learned scholar was his beloved friend; he gives a pleasing picture of the peaceful, simple life of More, and describes the highly affectionate manner of his life to his large family,—his wife, his son, and his wife's three daughters and their husbands, with eleven grand-children. Henry VIII. frequently visited him, besides various illustrious foreigners and scholars.

The MANOR OF CHELSEA is a very ancient one, and passed through many illustrious and noble hands. So far back as Edward the Confessor's

reign it was bestowed on the Abbot and Convent
of Westminster, by a charter, in the Saxon language. This charter is still preserved in the
British Museum. Several court rolls of this Manor
are preserved among the records of the Dean and
Chapter of Westminster. In one of these it is mentioned that "the wife of Phillip Wells was fined
sixpence for being a common babbler." Sir Reginald Bray was one of the earliest lords of this Manor.
He had been greatly instrumental in determining
Henry VII. to the throne: he obtained great honour
and wealth in consequence.

Henry VIII. possessed this Manor, and built a
beautiful Manor House for the use of his children.
In it his daughter Elizabeth passed part of her
youth under the care of the Queen Dowager,
Catherine Parr, and her husband, the celebrated and
unfortunate Duke of Somerset. Strange accounts
of the coarse conduct of the Duke to his young
charge have been handed down to us.

After the death of the Queen Dowager, it was
bestowed by Edward VI. on the Duke of Northumberland, who in Mary's reign was beheaded for
treason. His wife Jane was a singular instance of
the variations of fortune. She lost her husband
and one son on the scaffold; saw her other children
dispersed, while her property was confiscated, and
she reduced to poverty. Eventually the Queen was
successfully urged to reinstate her. She lived and
died in the Manor House, and left a remarkable
and long will. Her ladyship's magnificent tomb in
Chelsea Church has been described.

Ann of Cleves, who luckily for herself was only
divorced from Henry VIII., instead of losing her
head, also resided here some time, although she had
a palace at Lewes in Sussex, which is still shown
among the antiquities of that old town. Several
families of consideration held this old Manor and
house, but eventually it got into the noble family of
the Cheynes.

Sir Hans Sloane purchased the Manor of the last
Viscount Newhaven in the year 1712. Sir Hans
Sloane was one of those men who leave their mark
on the age in which they flourish. He was descended from a Scotch family, but educated in the
North of Ireland. He was an ardent botanist, of
no mean ability ; he studied the various branches of
physic successfully; was President of the Royal
College of Physicians; and was so great a benefactor of the botanical gardens at Chelsea, that he
greatly enriched them with scarce and curious
plants.

These gardens were the third of their kind in
England. The celebrated John Gerarde, the father
of English botany, established the first botanical
gardens in this country. The gardens of Trades-
cant, at South Lambeth, were the next. He collected a number of rare and curious plants. But
the whole were given, in 1667, to the University of
Oxford.

The BOTANICAL GARDENS at Chelsea are nearly
four acres in extent. Evelyn, that lover of trees
and gardens, mentions them in high terms in his
beautiful Diary. Various persons of ability managed

them, until they fell under the care of Petiver; he accumulated so large a collection of specimens of plants, &c., that after his death Sir Hans Sloane purchased it, and it was sent to the British Museum.

It was at these gardens that he first studied his favourite science. A statue of him, by the celebrated Rysbrach, in marble, stands in the centre. Sir Hans Sloane was physician to Queen Anne, and in her last illness he was called in; he was also the intimate friend of Sir Isaac Newton. He was created a Baronet by George the First, and was appointed Physician-General to the Army, being the first physician in England who had been thus rewarded. George the Second and his Queen placed entire confidence in his skill. When he purchased the Manor of Chelsea, he gave a large piece of ground to his favourite gardens, besides contributing in various ways to their embellishment. After Sir Isaac Newton's death, he was made President of the Royal Society.

He lived at Chelsea, in the Manor House, for some years, in elegant retirement; visited, however, by all the literary society of the day, including learned foreigners. Also, the Royal Family frequently paid him visits. He died in 1753, and was buried in the churchyard at Chelsea, with his lady. His magnificent tomb has been described.

Sir Hans Sloane may be said to have founded the British Museum; for his invaluable collection was sold at his death for £20,000., and was bestowed on that place, forming, as it were, the

nucleus for the present enormous collection. At
his death he divided the Manor of Chelsea between
two of his daughters,—one the wife of George
Stanley, Esq., and the other married to Lord Charles
Cadogan. The property still remains in the
Cadogan family. The eldest sons of the Earls of
Cadogan bear the title of Viscount Chelsea.

CHAPTER VI.

ITH respect to ancient houses, but few of them are left, and these chiefly by the water-side. Lindsay Row, Paradise Row, Church Street, and Cheyne Row contain the oldest houses now to be found in Chelsea. These were once the residences of remarkable characters. Sir Richard Steele, Dr. Hoadly, Dr. Smollett, Dr. Attenbury, Bishop of Rochester, and the Earl of Radnor were a few of the most noteworthy. The Earl of Radnor gave a sumptuous entertainment to King Charles in 1660, at a house in Paradise Row. It is but a shabby, mean-looking place now ; one wonders, in looking at the little squeezed-up houses, how accommodation was found for so many noble owners and their servants. But in it, however, lived for a large portion of their lives the Duke of St. Albans, the Duchess of Hamilton, the Earl of Pelham, and the Earl of Sandwich.

Dean Swift had only a lodging in Church Street, which, in a letter to " Stella," he thus mentions: " I got here with Patrick (his servant) and my portmanteau for sixpence, and pay six shillings a week for one silly room, with confounded coarse sheets." Dean

Atterbury, however, who had a house opposite, invited him to the run of his house and gardens.

House rent was not very high in Chelsea at that time, for Sir Richard Steele is mentioned in the parish accounts as paying fourteen pounds a year for his house in Paradise Row.

The celebrated Sir Theodore Mayne, physician to four kings—Henry IV.and Louis XIII. of France, and James I. and Charles I. of England—lived near the water-side. John Pym, the well-known member of the House of Commons in Charles the First's reign, and whose character and actions are matters of history, also resided here.

The Duchess of Mazarine, Charles the Second's beautiful mistress, had an elegant residence at Chelsea, near the water. Thither, of course, the King frequently went, taking all the fine gentlemen, courtiers, and wits of his court with him. Very grand musical entertainments, partly dramatic, were given by the Duchess; the performers being the most eminent that could be procured. It is believed that at these concerts the design of introducing the Italian Opera on the London boards was first suggested. In 1770 the opera of " Arsinoe" was performed at Drury Lane Theatre.

The Earl of Danvers had a mansion and park near the river side. It is now covered by mean streets, inhabited by denizens of the free-and-easy order.

WINCHESTER HOUSE, no longer standing, was the residence of eight Bishops of Winchester, who resided there successively after the Restoration of Charles II.

Mrs. Mary Astell, who was honoured by the friendship of Lady Hastings, (mentioned a few pages back), was a remarkable woman. Highly educated, she was mistress of the French and Latin languages, and a proficient in logic and philosophy; she spent nearly all her life at Chelsea, devoting it to literature, and wrote several remarkable works on religion and politics, and an Essay on the Female Sex, also an Address to them. She was the intimate acquaintance of all the eminent men of her time.

Sir Robert Walpole, Earl of Orford, who figures so conspicuously in the reigns of the two Georges, First and Second, had an elegant abode adjoining the Royal Hospital.

The once well-known DON SALTERO'S COFFEE HOUSE is still to be seen in Cheyne Walk. He lived there for a number of years, and had a large collection of curiosities, which were duplicates of some in the possession of Sir Hans Sloane, whose servant he had been. A humorous description of him and his collection may be seen in No. 34 of the *Tatler*.

Some very curious particulars have been related respecting the famous CHELSEA BUN HOUSE. It was rather a stylish cottage, with a well kept garden. George II., Queen Caroline, and the Princesses, bought buns here; as did also George III. and his family. It was so fashionable in the beginning of the last century, that on some Good Friday mornings no less than £250. has been taken for buns; and on the Good Friday of 1839 the prodigious number of 240,000 buns were sold. Were it not an accredited fact, this statement would appear incredible. Not only did royalty and the nobility and gentry think a "Chelsea bun" indispensable, but the working-classes, servants, shopmen, and others, who amused themselves in the Five Fields (on which Eaton and Belgrave Squares now stand) when their holidays occurred, considered a visit to the "Bun House" as absolutely necessary as a visit to Greenwich Fair was considered a short time since, when that fair existed.

There were other things at the Bun House which might have been attractive. It exhibited a collection of pictures (not first-rate), models, grotesque figures, and antiques. In the absence of "music halls," public cheap concerts, and other public places of amusement—so numerous in the present day—this place obtained a celebrity it would never have gained now.

The celebrated CHELSEA CHINA MANUFACTORY is a thing of the past. It was originally begun by a Mr. Sprimont, a foreigner. The particular kind of porcelain issued from this place has always been, and is now, highly valued. Even now that the produce of foreign manufactures are open to us, a genuine specimen of the "Chelsea china" always fetches a fancy price.

Of the old houses by the water-side, those in Cheyne Row, which were built in 1708, are the most imposing. There are several very high ones of a handsome description, one with gothic balconies, and its forecourt paved black and white; they have not been neglected, and are inhabited by highly respectable families. In these houses have lived a succession of those who were distinguished in their day for mental gifts or social advantages. Want of space, however, prevents the writer from dwelling at greater length on the character and circumstances of the remarkable persons whose residences rendered Chelsea so interesting and attractive for so long a period of its history. Like Hammersmith and Fulham, Chelsea had its Fishery, which was so lucrative and extensive as to be quite an institution. It gradually declined, however, from the same causes that destroyed the fisheries of the other two parishes.

The picturesque WOODEN BRIDGE, so attractive to artists, which crosses the river from Chelsea to Battersea, was built, or at least begun, in 1771, at a cost of £20,000. It is most inconvenient, and numbers of lives have been sacrificed. It is now, however, condemned, for a beautiful bridge is at last begun, to be called the " ALBERT BRIDGE." Chelsea may then be justly proud of its bridges ; more especially of that elaborate and very elegant suspension bridge, known as Battersea Bridge, but really belonging to Chelsea.

With respect to Churches, in addition to the Parish Church, Chelsea contains five others, of which the elegant CHURCH OF ST. LUKE's in Robert Street claims precedence. The Duke of Wellington laid the first stone on the 12th of October, 1820. It is built of Bath stone in the gothic style of the four-teenth century. From an elegant arcade in the front rises a beautiful and lofty tower, strengthened at the four corners by octagon-shaped buttresses, while the upper part is furnished with an open battlement. The altar window at the east end is very much admired. The nave and the two sides are separated by pointed arches and clustered columns. The roof is elegantly groined, and it is said, done in a style that has not been attempted even for three hundred years. The altar-piece is the entombing of Christ, very beautifully executed by Northcote, who had previously exhibited it at the British Institution in Pall Mall. The architect was Mr. James Savage. It has a crypt.

Among some good marble tablets to the memory of some highly respected inhabitants, is a very elegant monument by Chantrey, recording the death and services of the Hon. Henry Cadogan, who fell at the battle of Vittoria in 1813. It represents his soldiers lamenting the death of their beloved officer. His portrait is on a medallion, underneath is the Imperial Eagle of France, and at the top of the pillar supporting these is the letter N. This piece of sculpture is in Chantrey's best style.

Several members of the noble family of Cadogan are buried in a vault near the spot. In the Cemetery attached to it are buried some more of the late respected residents of the neighbourhood.

Christ Church, and St. Jude's, have little besides their usefulness to recommend them.

Trinity Church, Upper Chelsea, is rather elegant: it is of brick, but built and ornamented in the gothic style. Besides these there are two or three handsome Congregational Chapels, Roman Catholic and Nonconformist places of worship, and all these

have schools attached to them, which are flourishing.

Although a large portion of Chelsea consists of
mean, dirty houses, with a not very refined population roaming its streets, yet it contains many noble
streets of very handsome mansions and fine squares
inhabited by fashionable and aristocratic residents.

A great many extensive alterations which will really
be improvements are in progress, and when com-
pleted the modern Chelsea will be a handsome Town.

By the water side a handsome Boat Pier has been
erected—the CADOGAN PIER, with a handsome hotel,
the Cadogan Arms attached. Oakley Street, leading
from this spot to the King's Road, is a long street of
very good houses, both as to size and appearance.

The King's Road appears to be the most direct
thoroughfare through Chelsea. In the time of
Charles I. it was merely a footway used by the
gardeners and farmers to reach their lands. It
obtained the name of " King's Road " in the reign
of Charles II., who found it a convenient way of
getting to Hampton Court. From being a noted
place for robberies and murders, it has gradually
been built on, and at one time was highly attractive
for its beautiful nursery gardens. Even now there
are several large and flourishing places of this description : the Royal Exotic Nursery contains a
choice collection of rare Cape plants. The Ashburnham Park Nursery, and " Bull" Nursery, are
also well supplied with rare and valuable plants.

A handsome commodious building, the VESTRY
HALL, is in the King's Road. It is built in the

Italian style. Viscount Chelsea laid the first stone
in 1859. It contains ample and superior accommodation for vestry meetings, committees, and other
requirements of this busy and intelligent parish.
Paulton Square and Oakley Square are staid, respectable places, with some good houses.

Queen's Road obtained this name from an old white
house called "Queen Elizabeth's Larder," which had
stood there many years; it is now pulled down.
The Victoria Hospital, Chelsea Dispensary, the Hospital for Consumpton, the Cancer Hospital, are all
admirable institutions and beautiful buildings. The
two last, indeed, are not exactly in Chelsea; but as
they adjoin the parish so nearly, they are mentioned.

Sloane Square is at the end of the King's Road,
and now is merely a place of business; at one corner
is Grosvenor Bridge, once known as Blondel and
then as Bloody Bridge. It led to the Five Fields
on which those fine squares—Eaton and Belgrave
Squares—now stand. This place was remarkable
for murders and other outrages. Hence the signi-
ficant and horrible cognomen of "bloody" was
attached to the bridge and gate close to it. It was
a wooden bridge, of picturesque form, not above ten
or twelve feet wide, and spanned a narrow creek
opening from the Thames.

Hans Place is a collection of old fashioned houses.
It occupies the site of a beautiful estate called the
Pavilion, built by a gentleman of the name of
Holland for himself. That interesting poetess,
L. E. L., or Miss Landon, was born at number
twenty five in this place, and educated at number

twenty-two. The lady who kept the school was a literary lady of considerable acquirement and ability, Miss Bowden; she wrote some creditable works— "A Poetical Introduction to the Study of Botany," and the "Pleasures of Friendship." She afterwards married the Count St. Quentin.

Among Miss Landon's fellow-pupils were Miss Roberts, who wrote so many intelligent articles on India; Lady Caroline Lamb, who stabbed herself with a pair of scissors at a ball, for the sake of Lord Byron, who mentions her in his "Don Juan" as "having played the devil, and then wrote a novel." She certainly did write three romantic novels, and was afterwards the wife of Viscount Melbourne; she lived for some time at number twenty-two.

Miss Mitford, Lady Bulwer, and Mrs. S. C. Hall were partly educated by the same accomplished lady at number twenty-two; forming a galaxy of talent not often collected in one place. They were not all there at the same time, it is true; but a very short interval elapsed between them, and Miss Roberts was the intimate friend of L. E. L.

Miss Landon was very fond of this place, retiring to it with pleasure when anything called her away. It is a very dull place, and an ugly one; and yet here she wrote all her graceful productions. She usually sat in her sleeping-room, which was destitute of any thing at all ornamental. It is said that places produce or contribute to the making of geniuses. Now, nothing in Hans Place could suggest any poetical ideas or flights of fancy; but would have a tendency, one would think, to extinguish any feelings of this kind in their birth. So that places will not create talent, if nature has withheld all intellectual gifts.

CREMORNE HOUSE was built and the grounds laid out in an elegant style early in the eighteenth century by Theophilus Earl of Huntingdon, who died in the year 1746. Viscount Powerscourt was their next possessor, and successively this property fell to the Dowager Countess of Exeter and Sir Richard Lyttleton. He was the husband of the Dowager Countess of Bridgewater. He died in 1770, and her ladyship died in 1777. After their death Baron Dartry, Viscount Cremorne, purchased the estate. His lordship very considerably enlarged and beautified the house and estate, with the aid and skill of the eminent Mr. James Wyatt. He lived to the great age of 89, and was truly lamented for his enlarged generosity, and christian goodness. His lady, the Viscountess Cremorne, was born in Philadelphia. She resided for a large portion of every year at Chelsea, and was truly the Lady Bountiful of the place, being one of the kindest and most charitable residents in the parish. She kept a large establishment; exercising a liberal hospitality, not only to the rich, but frequently entertaining the poor in her elegant grounds. Her ladyship was highly respected, and like her lord she, too, was much lamented when she died in 1825. When residing at Cremorne House, a visit from Queen Charlotte was no unusual event. After her death Granville Penn, Esq., descended from the celebrated William Penn, resided here for a long time.

Eventually they fell into the hands of various proprietors, and are now the well known Cremorne Gardens. Everything has been done to render this once elegant place suitable for cockney tastes, but the gardens are still beautiful. Much has been said about the deterioration of Chelsea owing to these gardens. But although the idle and the dissolute throng there, so they do in all our public places and streets. Meantime a good deal of innocent amusement goes on there. They are refreshing and healthful, and command fine views over the river, and are still studded with fine old trees. Considering the class for whom chiefly these gardens have been arranged, the amusements are conducted with considerable decorum, while a great deal that is refining and instructive is set forth in pyrotechnical and occasionally zoological representations, and even the theatrical entertainments are on a par with the minor theatres of London.

HISTORICAL NOTICES.

Parish of Kensington.

Parish of Kensington.

CHAPTER I.

FROM the following description of Kensington it will be found that this parish has in no way deteriorated, but that from an early period it has been favoured not only (for some years of its history) by Royalty, but as being the residence of numbers of the nobility and gentry. In the present day, indeed, it has become a continuation of the "West End." It is a very large and important parish, boasting of a Royal Palace and Park, Holland House and grounds, a noble unique Museum, Horticultural Garden, as well as the Royal Albert Hall of Arts, shortly to be opened by Her Majesty the Queen. Exactly opposite to this is a Memorial to his Royal Highness the late Prince Albert. It is the most elegant of the numerous erections of this kind in the country. Kensington also contains a great many very fine old houses, and an abundance of noble modern mansions, the town houses of the aristocracy.

It has a much larger population than the other three parishes. In 1861 it showed the number of inhabitants to be 70,108, it is more than 100,000 now. No doubt when the particulars of the new census are published, as they will shortly be, the numbers will show a great increase.

Kensington lies on a bed of gravel from six to ten feet thick, sparsely covered by a rich dark loam that has been highly dressed. The air is not quite so mild as it is in the neighbouring parishes. It is more bracing and very pure and healthy. It is one mile and a half from Hyde Park Corner; the parish of Fulham bounds it on the south west; Chelsea and Hammersmith join it; towards Notting Hill and Bayswater, the land rises almost into the dignity of hills. It is a wide rambling parish, running from St. Margaret's, Westminster, to Paddington. It includes the districts of Earl's Court, the two Bromptons, old and new, the Gravel Pits, Kensal Green, Little Chelsea, or as now called West Brompton. All these places were once small villages, some of the parochial divisions are rather odd, for a few of the houses in Sloane Street, (which is in Chelsea) belong to this parish. Kensington Palace, and part of the High Street are in the parish of Westminster.

Between forty and fifty years ago, while the writer of these pages was living at Kensington, a great scandal, and no little merriment was occasioned by the circumstance of a poor wayfarer dropping down dead on the boundary line of the two parishes : his head lying in one parish, and his legs in the other, for some time neither of the two parishes would bury him. At length, however, the poor defunct was interred, the parishes dividing the expense between them.

Kensington once sent no small amount of hay, vegetables, and fruit to the London markets. But the vast amount of building that has been going on in the parish for the last twenty or thirty years, has gradually occupied the lands so long devoted to gardening and agriculture. This parish once abounded with mineral springs; there is one now in Kensington Gardens (St. Govan's Well), which is still resorted to and taken care of. In 1698 some of those wells were highly valued; more especially those at Notting Hill, where there was a house built for the purpose of dispensing the waters. For many years subsequently, they attracted a considerable number of the public, and were very fashionable. Some of these wells contained a large quantity of salts. The one in Kensington Gardens is chalybeate. Henry VIIIth's Conduit on Palace Green was once very celebrated. It had some curious buildings attached to it, called the Bell and Water Tower, built for the use of Queen Elizabeth when a child. The water in it has long been unfit for use. The brick-work around it has fallen partly in, some large shrubs have rooted themselves there, and it is now enclosed in the Barrack-yard, presenting in the summer a not unpicturesque clump of greenery.

The origin or derivation of the name of Kensington has been a matter of some dispute; but it seems to have been originally *Chenesiton*, and is thus mentioned in "Domesday Book." Various writers mention it as *Kensitune, Kensintunæ, Kingsington,* and eventually *Kensington.* The north part of this parish was once a portion of the great Middlesex Forest, which stretched away for miles on this side of London.

The MANOR OF KENSINGTON is ancient, and was held by the noble family of the De Veres, whose descendants with few exceptions were all brave soldiers and influential subjects. One of them was a Baron of the Magna Charta, and one commanded at the battles of Cressy and Poictiers, while another was conspicuous for his bravery at Agincourt. Another noble descendant was that great lord who entertained Henry the Seventh with such magnificence at his house, that he was fined for doing so at. a cost so evidently beyond his means. This family gave no less than twenty Earls of Oxford to the English Peerage.

The first Lord of this Manor was Bishop Constance, who came over with William the Conqueror, and Aubrey de Vere, who also came over in his train, held it of the Bishop. Eventually the Manor came wholly into the possession of the De Veres. One of the Earls of Oxford in 1526 dying without issue, it descended through various noble or knightly hands until it came to Sir Walter Cope, who in the reign of James the First built Holland House. Sir Walter Cope also held the Manors of Earl's Court and of West Town, as that part of Kensington contiguous to the Holland Estate was called.

Of the seven oldest and most interesting places

that Kensington boasts of, namely, Holland House, the Square, the Palace, the Gardens, the Church, Kensington House, and Campden House, two of them have disappeared. The Church has been pulled down, as it showed symptoms of giving way, but it will be replaced by a very handsome new one in progress of building; while Campden House was destroyed by fire a few years ago. Its destruction attracted much public attention. It had been heavily insured. The office that held the insurance disputed payment, but after an unpleasant litigation were obliged to satisfy the claim in full. It was a great loss to Kensington. It was so beautiful and interesting a place, and contained so many valuable paintings, besides numerous objects of art and vertu. The gardens also were very beautiful, and had been laid out with great taste.

CHAPTER II.

HE PARISH CHURCH of Kensington, although considered by the late Bishop Blomfield as the ugliest church in his diocese, was an interesting structure, on account of the historical reminiscences attached to it. It certainly was remarkably plain and unpretending, but it was a very comfortable, convenient, capacious erection ; and contained a good many monuments, which if not remarkable for their beauty, were interesting mementos of those who had been loved and honoured in their lives.

It stood on the site of a very ancient Saxon church. So far back as the reign of Henry I. it is mentioned that a Godfrey de Vere, to whom it belonged as lord of the manor, left it on his death-bed to the Monastery of Abingdon. Eventually it was placed under the patronage of the Bishop of London, in whose diocese it now is. The present, or rather the church that has lately been pulled down, was built in 1683 or 1684. The expense was defrayed by subscription. King William III., Princess Anne his daughter, the Bishop of London, and other noble persons, gave large sums towards the expenses of its erection.

It contained one hundred and fourteen monuments and tablets of various descriptions, but not
any of them so beautiful as those in Chelsea old
Church. The most considerable of these is a monument in white marble to the memory of the Earl of
Warwick, who died 1759, and his Countess, as also
their daughter, the Lady Charlotte Rich. The Earl
is represented as sitting, resting his arm on an urn,
and clothed in a *Roman* habit. Some of the tablets
affixed to the walls are handsome. All these mementos have been carefully removed, and will be
placed in the new church.

Kensington churchyard is a very pretty one. A
number of those graceful trees, the willow, are dotted
over it, and it contains a number of good monuments,
interspersed with flowers. Just at this particular
time that the new church is being built, it is of
course in disorder. But when that is finished, the
church and churchyard will be highly ornamental to
Kensington.

The churchyard is full of monuments to various
noble and remarkable persons, and on the outside
walls were various tablets, one of them to Viscount
Molesworth and his lady, dated 1819. Another
tablet records the death of James Elphinstone, who
lived at Kensington House, author of several trea-
tises on education, and who translated Martial. On
a flat stone is recorded the death of Francesco
Bianchi, the musical composer, and his infant
daughter. He died of grief for her loss. Sir Thomas
Meaulis, the celebrated Bacon's attached secretary,
was buried here. He raised a statue (still standing)

to his beloved master's memory, at St. Alban's. Another burial is that of a Sir Manhood Penruddock, remarkable only for the manner of his death. He fell in a duel, fought at Notting Wood in 1608 ; the place is near " Notting Hill." The father and grandfather of the two George Colmans', the dramatists, were here consigned to their last repose.

Under a flat stone lie the remains of Dr. John Jortin, author of the " Life of Erasmus," who was an elegant scholar and sound theologian. The Rev. Martin Madan, who startled the religious world by his book, entitled " Thelypthora, or Female Ruin," has a grave and stone to his memory. On the strength of the Mosaic law, he advocated polygamy as a remedy for immorality. He got into considerable disgrace by these opinions ; the more especially as they were advanced in strong, and rather too explicit language, considering the nature of the subject.

Mrs. Elizabeth Inchbald, who will never be forgotten while her two beautiful works of the " Simple Story" and " Nature and Art" are read, lies here ; not far from the grave of the learned and amiable Dr. Warren, a celebrated physician with whom she was secretly in love. It is said by one of her biographers that she used to pace Sackville Street, in Piccadilly, after dusk, merely to get a glimpse of him, if possible, through the blinds.

Spofforth, composer of so many beautiful glees, has a small tablet. James Mill, the historian of British India, is mentioned on a small tablet inside

the church. Several of the tombs and tablets have
long and well-written epitaphs, but all of them are
too long for quotation.

The old church had many interesting memories
attached to it.   Lord Holland and Wilberforce, so
extremely different in their principles, attended service regularly; surprising the Rev. Thomas Rimell,
when he officiated, by sitting in the same pew side
by side.   It was, indeed, a remarkable contrast, and
a very pleasing one.

Canning's grand and massive head was often seen
bowed in prayer.   He had a house for many years
at Kensington.   David Wilkie, who painted a great
many of his pictures at his residence in this place,
attended divine service; although the son of a
minister of the Kirk of Scotland.   Nassau Senior,
the well-known political economist, attended also,
although he lived at Hyde Park Gate.   Thackeray,
who planned and built a comfortable, good-looking
house on Palace Green, was often one of the con-
gregation.   Lord Macaulay, when he came to reside
at Holly Lodge, Campden Hill, lost no time in
securing himself a seat in the parish church, and
also obtaining a list of the parochial charities.   Con-
fined to the house in the winter by asthma, yet he
was regular in his attendance during the summer.

To go back for a century or so, Sir Isaac Newton,
while he lived in the place, was one of the wor-
shippers in the old church.   Lady Macdonald, who
resided in this parish for some years, was a devout
and regular attendant.   Her ladyship, however, is
only thus briefly mentioned as being the mistress

of that Flora Macdonald who was so instrumental
in aiding the escape of Prince Charles Edward, after
the unfortunate battle of Culloden.

Coke, the eminent agriculturist, had a pew in the
church.   He is celebrated for the introduction of
turnip husbandry into the county of Norfolk, where
it has quite altered the face of the country, and been
productive of vast benefit.

CHAPTER III.

ENSINGTON PALACE is a remarkably plain, solemn pile of red brick buildings; large, and no doubt extremely comfortable in its interior arrangements. It has, however, been rendered an interesting place by those who have resided in it. Her present Gracious Majesty was born and passed her early youth in it. The place was first mentioned in the parish books in 1651, as the property of Sir Heneage Finch. It was then much smaller than it is now. After Sir H. Finch had been raised to the peerage as Earl of Nottingham, it was called Nottingham House. Daniel, the second Earl of Nottingham, sold it to King William the Third. It then became the "Royal Palace of Kensington." The various monarchs who have lived in it made many important additions and alterations. Part of it was arranged by Sir Christopher Wren. The Palace is now of considerable extent; it consists of three courts,—the clock court, the prince's court, and the princess's court. It has also extensive buildings for domestic uses, and a large long building built by Queen Anne for a ball-room, but used until lately as a green house.

Although the Palace stands in extensive park-like

grounds, yet its present inhabitants have no private gardens. They are open to the public, and surrounded on all sides by a large population, who traverse its stately walks and avenues from morning till night. It is a matter of surprise, indeed, that no portion of the grounds have been rendered exclusive; especially as there is always one or more members of the Royal Family residing in it. The grounds are also too full of trees, which have in consequence grown up weak and thin, and there are very few large trees there.

The Palace was a favourite abode of Royalty for about two centuries; a circumstance that has rendered Kensington the fashionable, aristocratic place it is. The tide of prosperity and fashion set in to it when William came to reside here, and has never since receded. His Majesty, indeed, was very fond of the place, and found considerable relaxation from his public duties, when he could retire with his Queen and some select friends. A great many important Councils however were held here, and many interesting occurrences of his reign happened during his residence in it. In this palace he breathed his last.

Queen Anne and her husband Prince George of Denmark succeeded his Majesty, and were also extremely attached to Kensington, and they also died here. King George the First came next. During his reign the interior of the Palace was much improved. The cupola room was built, and the chief staircase decorated in a handsome manner. George the First, however, died at Osnaburgh.

When George the Second came to the throne, his favourite residence was Kensington Palace; his Majesty and his consort Queen Caroline were both delighted with its situation, and the genial air of the place. The Queen expended large sums in improving the palace and grounds, and, being fond of society, handsome entertainments were given in a magnificent style; while she held a Court regularly every Sunday after divine service. During the residence of this royal couple, Kensington became very attractive and fashionable. They also both died here.

A large and valuable collection of pictures once ornamented the galleries and rooms of the Palace; but they have been removed some time since and distributed.

Since the death of George II. and his consort, there are always some high members of the Royal family who either reside here wholly, or use it as their town residence. At present their Royal Highnesses the Prince and Princess of Teck reside here when in town.

CHAPTER IV.

LTHOUGH CAMPDEN HOUSE is no longer
standing, it was so well known and admired,
and so many persons doubtless remember it,
that perhaps a short account of it may be acceptable.
It was built by Sir Baptist Hicks in 1612. Formed
of brick, with stone mullions and quoins, it was of
no decided order of architecture, but still it was
picturesque and quaint.

The interior was very handsome : the hall wains-
coted with veined oak. The great dining-room
was a truly beautiful room, the wainscot was so
richly carved ; the mantel-piece was an elaborate
piece of sculpture, called the Tabernacle mantel,—
six beautiful columns supported a pediment. Between the columns were various grotesque devices.
Two nearly life-size human figures supported this
imposing structure, while the whole was ornamented
in a unique, if quaint, yet most effective style. It
was, indeed, a beautiful specimen of the arts of the
time it was erected in. Some of the fine rooms in
the house were ornamented with stuccoed ceilings,
and otherwise decorated with richly-carved wains-
cots and mantel-pieces. Added to these, the whole
house was furnished in the most elegant manner,

and enriched with fine pictures and numerous articles of vertu.

Queen Anne lived here for five years, and the house was then enlarged and beautified for her residence. It was called Campden House after the first Viscount Campden. He was the son of Sir M. Hicks, a silk mercer of London : he was advanced to the Peerage in 1628. After his death, his son-in-law, Lord Noel, resided here. The Noel family possessed the house until Queen Anne came to Kensington for the benefit of the air for her little son the Duke of Gloucester. LITTLE CAMPDEN HOUSE, which is still standing, was built, it is said, to accommodate her Majesty's household. Queen Anne hired the house of the Noel family. Various noble persons occupied this fine mansion. Eventually it became the property of Stephen Pitt, Esq., a wealthy parishioner. At length, a few years ago, it was, with all its rich and beautiful works of art, totally destroyed by fire. Another large house, in very good taste, has been erected on its site. It is not, however, inhabited. The garden has been neglected, and is at present nothing more than a piece of waste ground : some fine trees standing there give it a melancholy appearance, attesting so plainly to its by-gone beauty.

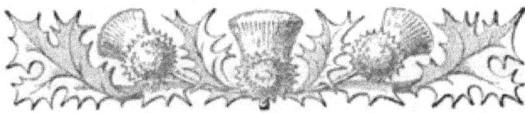

CHAPTER V.

OLLAND HOUSE is the largest and most interesting mansion to be found near the Metropolis. It is well known to nearly all the civilized world; for a large amount of political interest is attached to it, from having been the residence of such celebrated statesmen. It is not remarkable for its beauty; but it has a particularly venerable, quaint appearance, and attracts numerous visitors. Even foreigners of any taste for ancient localities go to see " Holland House." It stands in a very pleasing situation, on a slight eminence, surrounded by its gardens and park; for although a large portion of the Holland estate is now built upon, yet a considerable portion of the park is left, and is laid out with so much taste that it is very beautiful.

Near the house, at the back, are some very large old cedar trees, and one magnificent elm, which measures, at a yard from the ground, nineteen feet round. A portion of the grounds in front are elegantly laid out in the Italian style, interspersed with green alleys, and fences of trees trimmed to form arches.

All the turf about these grounds has been so well

kept that it forms a luxurious green carpet at all
times of the year, and many secluded nooks may be
found in the park,—an agreeable feature which is
not a little surprising, considering it is not more
than two miles from Hyde Park Corner.   Near the
house is an arbour dedicated to Rogers the poet,
with a long copy of verses by Luttrell, and a very
neat couplet by the late Lord Holland.

> " Here Rogers sat, and here for ever dwell,
>   To me those pleasures that he sang so well."

A tradition, (which is not positively established,
however,) belongs to the meadow in front of the
house.   It is said that Cromwell and Ireton held a
consultation in the middle of it, being thus secure
from listeners.

A bust of Napoleon in the grounds is inscribed
with a quotation from Homer.   It has been thus
translated :

> " He is not dead, he breathes the air,
>   In lands beyond the deep ;
> Some distant sea-girt island, where,
>   Harsh men the hero keep."

In Aubrey's " Miscellanies" is another interesting
tradition attached to the gardens.   Lady Diana
Rich, the beautiful daughter of one of the Lords
Holland, met the apparition of herself, dress and all,
at the unromantic hour of eleven in the forenoon.
One month afterwards she died of the small-pox,

After such an occurrence, of course her ladyship's
ghost used to frequent the place.   But as ghosts in

these prosaic days no longer visit us, the place is now free from these interesting visitors.

In these gardens was grown the earliest specimen of that now well known flower the dahlia. It had been brought from Spain by Lord Holland.

Holland House was built about the latter end of the 16th century by Sir W. Cope, after the designs of John Thorpe, an architect of some ability. It is formed of the usual red brick so much in vogue at that time, with stone dressings. The outside has such a venerable time-worn appearance, that it looks much older than it is, and offers the only appearance of antiquity it has; for the interior has been by its successive residents much altered and completely modernized. It is elegantly fitted up and adorned with beautiful pictures, statues, statuettes, and busts. These are so numerous, that a mere list of them would form a tolerably sized catalogue.

The upper part of Holland House overlooks extensive views. The back commands some pleasing scenery of the Surrey hills, while the front overlooks those of Hampstead, Harrow, and Highgate.

The first noble inhabitant of Holland House was Henry Rich, Earl of Holland, who married Isabella, daughter and heiress of Sir Walter Cope. It came into his possession, therefore, in right of his wife. His lordship's mother was the "Sacharissa" of that elegant, excellent, and gallant gentleman Sir Phillip Sydney, whose graceful pen has recorded her attractions.

Lord Holland, after passing a gay and sparkling

life, and entertaining all the rank, fashion, and celebrities of the time, was put to death in the civil
wars; and like the fop that he was, he went to the
scaffold in a white satin waistcoat and cap, the latter
trimmed with silver lace.

General Fairfax occupied the house a few months
afterwards. At the Restoration the house reverted
to its rightful owners. Part of the time from the
Restoration to the Georges, first and second, the
house was let on short leases, and even as apart-
ments for lodgers. Among these temporary residents
were some remarkable persons. The first Earl of
Annesley, who obtained the title from Charles II.
as a reward for his services; Sir John Chardin, the
well known traveller, who was made a knight by the
same monarch; the Duchess of Buckinghamshire,
illegitimate daughter of James II. Her whimsical
ladyship was a star of some magnitude in her time.
Bishop Atterbery also lived here a short time. But
the most interesting and illustrious of these temporary lodgers was the celebrated William Penn,
who was even then so famous, and his visitors so
numerous, that on some occasions no less than two
hundred persons would be waiting to greet this the
future founder of the now great state of Pennsyl-
vania in America. He can only in this place be
thus briefly alluded to; although his character,
actions, and life merit a more particular notice.
They are, however, set forth and described by able
pens in other works. Shipper, the famous Jacobite,
sojourned for a time here.

The second Earl of Holland lived so quietly here

that the only interesting circumstance connected
with him is, that his son Edward, who succeeded
him not only in the title of Earl of Holland, but as
fifth Earl of Warwick (in consequence of a failure of
heirs in the elder branch), married a daughter of
Sir Thomas Myddelton, who, when a widow, married Addison. He was tutor to one of her sons.
Addison's residence bestowed undying interest on
the old house. The green lane that he used to
pace in his meditations is now the Addison Road,
and large handsome villas line it, filled with wealthy
and aristocratic tenants.

It was to her son, the Earl of Warwick, that
Addison is said to have spoken those memorable
words attributed to him when dying, "See how a
Christian can die."

After Addison's death the house remained in the
possession of the Warwick family until it was sold
to Henry Fox, who afterwards became the first Earl
Holland of the Foxes. He was no mean orator,
and remarkably addicted to all the pleasures of this
world; and being blessed with particularly good
health, vigour, and wealth, his life was more full of
unbroken enjoyment than falls to the lot of the
majority. He married a daughter of the Duke of
Richmond under romantic circumstances, for he
eloped with her. His marriage also was a very
happy one.

Holland House was rendered still more notable
by the residence, during his youth, of the celebrated
Charles Fox. The house has been for some years,
and is now, in the possession of the Foxes.

CHAPTER VI.

THE old houses and other interesting places have now to be noticed. The most conspicuous of these is KENSINGTON HOUSE, at the beginning of the High Street, coming from London. It may here be observed that, of the four parishes, Kensington has the best approaches to it. The road from Hyde Park Corner to the town is really a beautiful drive or walk, especially coming from Knightsbridge. Hyde Park and the Gardens on one side, and the other bordered by large, imposing, and some of them beautiful mansions.

Kensington House was built about two hundred years ago, of handsome red brick, with stone facings and dressings. It is very wide, and not very high, and from some reason or other shows no sign of age; looking so fresh, it is difficult to believe that this remarkable looking house *is* old. It was built by a member of the Noel family, some of whom resided here. Charles II. was a frequent visitor to his beautiful mistress, the Duchess of Portsmouth. She had been the charming Louise de Queroailles, and lived here for a long time. Somewhere about 1753, James Elphinstone opened a school here. He was not only an excellent man, of a simple pious character, but also a scholar of considerable attainments, and an able, intelligent teacher. He was also an author. One of his works was rather remarkable. " Propriety ascertained in her picture, or English speech and spelling rendered mutual Guides." It was an attempt, and an unsuccessful one, to alter the entire system of etymology. He was much respected, and visited by many distinguished persons, while Dr. Johnson and the celebrated Franklyn were his intimate friends. Among his scholars was the late Mr. Shiel. After Elphinstone's death, the house was opened as a boarding house. The charming Mrs. Inchbald lived here for about two years, and here she died. The house is now a private lunatic asylum.

In the beginning of the present century most of the roads were very different to what they are now. Among the very worst of them was the road from Hyde Park Corner to Kensington. It was at times nearly impassable from mud and holes, which rendered it very dangerous. The worst part of it was THE GORE, this name being bestowed upon that place as being particularly muddy. The road is now as smooth as a bowling green. At this place has been erected quite a little town of handsome houses, none of them very old, but remarkable and interesting persons have rendered this spot attractive. KINGSTON, or as once, ENNISMORE HOUSE, was built by the Duchess of Kingston who makes such a disreputable appearance in history. She was a beautiful bold woman, who used to swear; and frequent public places, dressed so scantily as to be

nearly in a state of nudity. On one occasion she
went to a msquerade dressed, or rather not dressed,
as Eve. She married twice—first, a boy in his
teens, the Marquis of Bristol; secondly, a man old
enough to be her father, the Duke of Kingston.
There are a few old houses at the UPPER GORE which
are very interesting. They are not large, but they
speak so plainly of former respectability and fashion,
and are so well preserved and tenanted by highly
respectable families, that, contrasted as they are
with the showy modern erections in their immediate
neighbourhood, they forcibly arrest the attention.
Small and narrow, and possibly inconveniently so
inside, some well-known persons resided there.
Mrs. Inchbald lodged at number two. Wilkes the
democrat, the pious Wilberforce, and Count d'Orsay
lived in one or other of them for a part of their
lives. The late Hon. Miss Eden also lived and
died there. She was the authoress of two well-
known works of fiction, and published many entertaining letters from India.

GORE HOUSE, so well known to all the Literati and
fashion of the day, when inhabited by Lady Blessington and Count d'Orsay, has been removed. On
its site stands the ROYAL ALBERT HALL OF ARTS.
It was first occupied by a Government contractor of
such mean propensities that the memory of his miser-
like habits remains yet. Wilberforce lived there for
some time. The next was Lady Blessington, about
whom it is unnecessary, interesting as her life and
character is, to give any information, as no doubt the
readers of these pages are well acquainted with

them. The last inhabitant of this once-elegant
house was Monsieur Soyer, of gastronomical fame.
He opened the house as a large Restaurant for the
million during the year of the Great Exhibition.

KENSINGTON NEW TOWN, as it is called, consists
of handsome streets and houses, and lies at the back
of the road to London. It occupies the place of
green fields and nursery gardens, once so numerous
in this parish. There are a few of them left, but
much contracted in size.

KENSINGTON HIGH STREET has been rendered as
much like a London street as smart handsome shops
can make it. But it still resembles a country town.
The houses are not all of the same height or width,
and hardly two of them alike. There are some fine
old houses left standing about the town. One of them,
COLBY HOUSE, in the High Street, was built by a
miser, Sir Thomas Colby, a Commissioner in the
Victualling Office, in 1720. Of penurious habits, he
amassed a large fortune, and was created a baronet.
Going down one night from his warm bed to secure
the key of the wine cellar, which he had forgotten,
he caught a cold, which killed him. At his death,
his fortune was divided between six day labourers,
his only relatives.

About the middle of the High Street is a turning
leading to some mean houses, calculated to accommodate a few hundreds. Nevertheless, a colony of
one thousand of the lower orders of Irish are located
here. The reader may imagine the state of things.
Fortunately for the town they are (for Irish people)
tolerably quiet. Efforts have been made to remove

them. The existence of a place like this in aristocratic Kensington is rather surprising. On the opposite side of the way is a Pastry-cook's, remarkable for being the very oldest establishment of this kind in or near London. Cobbett's house and garden, in which he took such pride, is now a candle manufactory. Kensington Square contains some large noble houses of a melancholy aspect, owing to their being built in a fashion now gone by. The square was built in the reign of James II., and until lately was inhabited by high and celebrated persons, and for a hundred years or so was as fashionable a place as any of the London squares are at this time. The famous Duchess of Mazarine, niece of Cardinal Mazarine, was the first character of note who resided here. Various accounts record her taking evening walks, surrounded by French noble gallants and her faithful admirer and friend, St. Evremond. That curious character, author of books which few can wish to read—Sir Richard Blackmore, Physician to William III.—had a house in this place. Three prelates, whose characters are noteworthy, dwelt here for some time : Hough, Bishop of Winchester ; Herring, Bishop of Bangor, who contributed some excellent letters to that well known educational work, " Elegant Epistles," with Bishop Mawson, thus bestowing no small amount of clerical dignity on the place. It is very respectably inhabited at the present time. But the new railway station in the town being so near to it, and the pulling down so many houses, has rendered the approaches to it now so very disagreeable that it is difficult to say what this fine old place will come to. There is an ancient Bluecoat School in the town, and a very handsome Vestry Hall. The Phillimore Terraces, Upper and Lower, Bath Terrace, and Earl's Court Terrace, are all old-fashioned solemn looking places, that contrast very oddly with the new-fashioned showy style of architecture of the present day.

The most interesting house in the town lies at the back of the High Street. BULLINGHAM HOUSE, in which Sir Isaac Newton resided for two years, on account of an illness. In 1726 he came to this place again; and here he died, in the eighty-fourth or eighty-fifth year of his age, possessed of a large fortune, and unmarried. Bullingham House is now used as a high-class seminary for young ladies. An iron plate on the wall commemorates the circumstance of his residence here.

The OLD VICARAGE is not far off, and several fine old houses are close by, all standing in such odd positions and shut up in such high walls, that this part of Kensington is certainly the oddest nook in the place. Holland Street and Church Street join at one corner. They are both old-fashioned places, although Church Street is a very busy one. The road takes a violent twist just here, and what with the extreme narrowness of the pavement, nothing can be more dangerous. One wonders why some improvement is not made. Kensington is remarkable for containing within its bounds three such large places of recreation and intellectual amusement as the Horticultural Gardens, the South Kensington Museum, and now the HALL OF ARTS.

This noble building is much admired. There is nothing in any part of London on so large a scale. The whole building forms an elliptical oval, with three handsome porches; it is two hundred and seventy-two feet long, by a width of two hundred and thirty-eight feet. It extends from the Kensington Road to the Horticultural Gardens, with which it is connected; it is elegantly formed of coloured bricks, which were made at Fareham, in Hampshire, and tastefully decorated with terra cotta, designed and executed by Messrs. Gibbs and Cumming of Tamworth. A very handsome frieze runs around the dome, divided into seven compartments, containing allegorical designs commemorative of the Great Exhibition. These have been furnished by numerous able artists, and are very beautiful. The iron roof was supplied by the Engineering Company, and Lieut.-Colonel Scott was the architect. Inside, the arrangements are at once elegant and commodious. The Arena is at the bottom, in the centre of the Hall; surrounding this, is the Amphitheatre, arranged in ten rows of chairs. These last are made on a novel and most convenient plan; being made to revolve on a central iron leg screwed to the floor. Thus the occupant of a chair can give it a half turn, and so allow late arrivals to pass to their seats without rising. The back seats of the Amphitheatre are arranged into Loggia boxes; next comes the Grand Tier of boxes. The boxes intended for her Majesty the Queen, and for the Prince of Wales, are on this tier. There is yet another tier of boxes, and above these the Balcony. Higher still is the Picture

Gallery, which has not only seats for two thousand persons, but is wide enough for a promenade ; several doors open from this to an outside balcony. So the promenaders can take the air when they choose, by walking on the flat roofs of the building.

The Hall is calculated to accommodate from six to eight thousand persons. It is one hundred and thirty-five feet high, and is surmounted by a domed skylight of painted glass, with an opening in the centre to admit of a large star of gas burners. Besides this star, there are thirty clusters of one hundred and five jets suspended from various parts of the roof.

The orchestra will accommodate one thousand performers. The organ was built by Mr. H. Willis. It is sixty feet wide and seventy feet high, and contains nine thousand pipes ; some of them the largest ever made. The whole of the interior is in good taste, while the scagliola columns of the picture gallery have been much admired.

The floors are comfortably covered by dark red cocoa-nut matting ; no less than nine thousand yards having been used for this purpose.

In one most important respect, the Albert Hall will be a model for all buildings intended for large gatherings of the public. Spacious corridors run round on every floor, and are connected with twenty-two wide staircases ; and there are nineteen doors for exit and entrance. So that in the event of any real danger, or during any of those extraordinary panics which occasionally occur in places of this kind, the whole building might be safely vacated in less than ten minutes.

Exactly opposite to the Hall, across the Kensington Road, stands the ALBERT MEMORIAL, which, when completely finished, will be certainly one of the most elegant erections in or near London. It is fashioned as an open shrine for a life-size figure of his Royal Highness Prince Albert. The shrine stands on a pedestal of the purest and hardest Sicilian marble ever brought to this country. On its four sides have been carved nearly one hundred and eighty figures, life-size. These form a kind of panorama, representing the special Fine Arts which his Royal Highness did so much to encourage. The south side, facing the Hall, is devoted to Music and Poetry. On the north, Sculpture is represented; while the east and west sides illustrate Painting and Architecture. The life-size figures representing these Arts are not allegorical; but accurate and elaborate portraits of those great geniuses of all ages and nations, who were known to the world as Painters, Poets, Musicians, and Architects. The Albert Memorial, therefore, will not only be very beautiful, but also the most remarkable and interesting object in England; if not in Europe. The architect is G. G. Scott, Esq. At the four corners are to be placed four groups of white marble figures, representing the four quarters of the world. It is not nearly finished, and this description is necessarily imperfect. It stands in an elegant garden, and, with the Albert Hall, will make two magnificent objects, and still further ornament the already fine approach to Kensington.

KENSINGTON GARDENS.—There does not appear to be any authentic account of these Gardens, as to who originally planned them, or when this was done. But when King William the First purchased the house now called Kensington Palace from Sir Heneage Finch, it is mentioned that the extent of the gardens was about twenty-six acres, and laid out in the formal style prevalent at that time. When Queen Anne came to reside at Kensington, her Majesty greatly improved and altered them. It remained, however, for Queen Caroline, consort of George the Second, to give the Gardens their present pleasing appearance. Nearly three hundred acres of land were obtained from Hyde Park. Bridgeman, the landscape gardener, was employed to plant and lay them out. At one time a few rare trees and shrubs were planted; now that the Gardens are thrown open to the public all these have disappeared.

The Gardens are divided from Hyde Park by means of a fosse and low wall, almost level with the ground. This is a good contrivance, for it makes the Gardens appear so much larger. Although Hyde Park is not in Kensington Parish, yet a few words respecting it may be acceptable.

HYDE PARK is ancient; it was once the Hyde Farm of the Monastery of Westminster. At the Reformation it fell into the possession of the Crown, and became one of the Royal Parks. George Roper was the first keeper, and he had sixpence a-day for his services. Various knightly and noble persons afterwards held this office, which gradually came to

be of some value. During the usurpation of Cromwell, Hyde Park was put up to sale in three lots.
At the Restoration, King Charles the Second made
his brother, the Duke of Gloucester, Keeper of Hyde
Park. At this time it was well stocked with fruit
trees. A Mr. Hamilton was the next keeper, and
he let it out in Farms. But in 1670 it was enclosed
with a wall, and stocked with deer. The SERPEN-
TINE RIVER, which is so great an ornament to it
and to Kensington Gardens, was formed partly
under the influence of Queen Caroline. All the
springs, conduits and water-courses about the Park
were made to run into the bed that was dug for the
purpose, at an expense altogether of about nine
thousand pounds. Hyde Park was the scene of
many a conflict between the Royalists and Roundheads. The latter threw up two large forts with
four bastions each; one opposite ST. GEORGE's
HOSPITAL, and the other close to Mount Street.
The Park has also been the scene of some extraordinary gatherings and grand reviews.

BAYSWATER closely adjoins the Gardens. It was
once a pretty village at the top of the hill, and known
as " Bayard's Watering Place." It is remarkably
invigorating and healthy, and seems to be a favoured
spot. For it is built all over, and with large handsome houses and squares. NOTTING HILL, adjoining
Bayswater, is equally as favoured. About fifty years
since, this large populous place was a large farm on
the top of the hill, from whence some very fine views
were obtainable.

No remarkable historical event ever happened in

Kensington. Nevertheless, about fifty years ago, Kensington and Hammersmith were witnesses of very painful scenes; a description of which, it is hoped, will not be handed down to posterity. While that misguided and unhappy lady, Caroline, Consort of George the Fourth, was residing at Brandenburgh House—the once very elegant residence of the celebrated Margravine of Anspach—Kensington and Hammersmith were kept in a constant state of unseemly excitement. All the various London trades, and even some of the Guilds, made processions, with the various insignia of their callings, to offer addresses to her. The inhabitants of these two parishes took a decided and demonstrative part in the extraordinary and unhappy disputes of the Royal pair, and protected, as far as they could, the poor lady who lived so near them: for Brandenburgh House, which is now pulled down, stood in beautiful grounds between Hammersmith and Kensington, at the back of the road running through the two places. At her death, matters, in Kensington at least, reached their climax. Orders had been given that her remains were not to pass through the Parks, and that the Hearse should go up Church Street, and along the Bayswater Road. The Kensingtonians, however, determined that this programme should be altered. The stones were grubbed up, and two waggons were capsized across the entrance, rendering it impossible to take any vehicle up the street. Understanding that, unless haste was made, the Park gates would be closed by the military, the Hearse containing poor Caroline's body *galloped* through the town as fast as the horses could go. Chance stones had been flung about at the soldiers. One of them had struck the coachman on the back of his head, and as the hearse *tore along* blood was running down his back. After all, the Hearse did get through the Park, although a man was *shot dead* at one of the gates; but it was not until London was quite cleared that the funeral cortége was able to go along in the usual decorous manner on its way to Harwich, being reverently received at all the churches and resting-places on the way.

HISTORICAL NOTICES.

Parish of Fulham.

FULHAM CHURCH

Revd R. G. BAKER. M. A. Vicar.

Parish of Fulham.

CHAPTER I.

THE Parish of FULHAM is of an ancient date. So far back as 691 it is mentioned in a grant of the manor by Tyrhtilus Bishop of Hereford, to Erkenwald Bishop of London, as *Fulanham*.

Camden derives the name of *Fulham* from the Saxon word *Fullonham*, or the home of water fowls. Fulham once included Hammersmith, then a hamlet. It is now like Hammersmith, a London suburb. It is in the archdeaconry of Middlesex and diocese of the Bishop of London. It lies like its neighbour, on the north bank of the Thames; is in the jurisdiction of the Central Criminal Court, and of the Metropolitan Board of Works, and is in the South Western Postal District. Its population in 1861 was 15,589.

This parish is about five miles and a half long, and nearly two miles wide. The THAMES forms its southern bonndary, and the views in passing down the river in this part of its course, are very soft and

G

pleasing. From Chelsea. to Chiswick (about five
miles,) a constant succession of charming objects
gratify the eye of taste. The fine old houses on
Chiswick Mall, Chiswick Church, the Bishop's
Palace ; the quaint old bridge of Fulham, the
Churches of Fulham and Putney, exactly alike, and
exactly opposite to each other, and views of the
Surrey Hills, form a succession of pleasing and
picturesque scenery that attracts many visitors.
The rivers of the Dove, the Trent, the Avon, and
the Wye, are all remarkable for special lovely
scenery of their own ; but in few places in England
is there such a soft, dream-like beauty spread over
the scenery as pervades the banks of the Thames
from Hammersmith to Kingston.

A great quantity of fish was once caught, year by
year, and sent to the London markets. The sale,
indeed, was so considerable, that in the seventeenth
century the fisheries were leased to Sir Nicholas
Crispe and others for three salmons a-year.

A very cruel custom prevailed here and at Hammersmith. The Jews used to give a good price for
fishes scales to manufacture false pearls with. The
fishermen caught the *white* fish, and of those not
large enough for sale, they scraped the scales from
their backs, and tossed them in the river again to
die in torture. But as the fish left the river this
custom, together with the fisheries, gradually ceased.

In the Thames near Fulham Bridge is a shifting
sand-bank, well known to builders and others for
yielding a constant supply of sand peculiarly adapted
for mixing with lime for building purposes. This

sand may be useful, but lying where it does, it renders the navigation difficult if not dangerous.

The air of Fulham is very soft and pure; this, together with the rich alluvial soil, so liberally spread over the greater part of its lands, renders this parish so very favourable to the growth of all kinds of garden produce, of fruit trees, and flowers, that for ages it has sent large supplies of these articles to the London markets. A large quantity of asparagus of a superior kind is grown in this place, and is duly valued in the markets to which it finds its way.

Fulham, notwithstanding that bricks and mortar have made their usual encroachments on some of its green places, is a pleasant rural place. There are numbers of fine trees, large gardens, and the estate belonging to the Bishop's Palace, offering such a beautiful walk along the bank that confines the moat.

The older part of Fulham has been so little altered that it still retains the characteristics of a country town; of an aristocratic description, however, for it was once the favourite resort of the higher classes, and even now numbers a great many families of consideration amongst its inhabitants. A paucity of omnibuses and cabs, and the Railway Station being, as these places so often are, inconveniently situated, keeps the little town very quiet.

So much of this parish is laid out in market and fruit gardens that it offers numerous healthful walks.

It is true that there is nothing at all picturesque in the arrangements and appearance of market gardens; yet at the proper seasons, fields of flourish-

ing green vegetables, and trees loaded with handsome fruit, are pleasing objects, and the wind blows
freely and freshly over them.

In a place so favourable to the production of
flowers and fruits, there are many nursery gardens.
Of these the largest and best known is the Fulham
Nursery and Botanical Gardens, established about a
hundred years ago, the various proprietors have
carried it on with vigour and liberality. At these
gardens were exhibited the first Cork tree, the Cham-
pion oak, and the Bengal oak, all beautifully grown
splendid individuals of their kind. Here also was
seen the first Magnolia Grandiflora, the original
parent of the large plants to be seen in our various
conservatories.

The institution of Parishes is very ancient. Man-
kind being of sociable habits, it naturally followed
that collections of dwelling places were found to be
agreeable and convenient. To these the word
Parish has been applied from ancient times. Bishop
Honorios, who lived in the beginning of the seventeenth century, is said to have introduced this arrange-
ment into England.

In Domesday Book the divisions and bounds of
our parishes are described; and with few variations
the bounds and divisions are the same now.

In the primitive ages, parishes were patriarchal
in their character. The Lord of the Manor and the
Rector were looked up to: the former as chief whose
will was law, and the latter as a father whose spiritual
admonitions it were well to obey; and in many
respects a parish resembled a large family. Very

kindly relations and feelings existed between the rich
and poor of a parish. The latter took all their grie-
vances to the former, being sure of the requisite
amount of sympathy, assistance, and advice; these
things are greatly altered now, and not for the better.
This alteration, however, is chiefly among the inferior
classes. The rich and noble of the present day do
still sympathise with and help their poorer brethren,
and that most liberally. But that loving feeling of
homely respect is no longer felt or displayed by the
poor and the working portion of a parish towards
their superiors. A multitude of pernicious cheap
publications, and also the vast increase of the
various populations, has destroyed these feelings.
The cheap publications have taught them to *think*,
and to think *improperly*. While the immense populations of our time divides the social system into a
variety of classes unknown to our forefathers; in
whose experiences there were but two; the rich and
the poor. The higher classes of the present day,
to their honor be it asserted, do all they can to
revive these kindly relations; but it is only in
parishes remote from London influence that anything like the old homely devotion is at all under-
stood. Of course all the parishes in the London
district have long lost all feelings of the kind.

CHAPTER II.

ULHAM PARISH CHURCH stands at no great distance from the water. It has been built of stone in the decorated English style, and parts of it are ancient. It has a lofty and handsome tower at one end, supposed to have been erected in the fourteenth century. But even this is not all of the same period; for, in consequence of a storm which injured it in 1798, some modern battlements have been substituted for those that were thrown down by the winds. Antiquarian writers vary in their accounts of the exact period it was erected in. It has ten very beautiful bells. Some of them have curious inscriptions; on the sixth bell is written, "John Ruddle cast us all." On the tenth,—

" I to the church the living call,
    And to the grave I summons all."

It is dedicated to " All Saints."

Fulham is now a vicarage, and always in the gift of the Bishops of London. The earlier parish registers have been lost; of those remaining, they commence in 1679, but a large register book of benefactions, neatly written on vellum, begins in 1622. The book opens with a beautiful prayer, and contains a long list of bishops, noblemen, and various pious persons, who bequeathed money and lands to the poor of Fulham and Hammersmith, these two places being in one parish at that time.

Among the "items" of the "Churchwardens' Accounts" is a curious one relating to hats or caps. By a law passed in the reign of Elizabeth, every male person older than seven was obliged to wear a woollen hat or cap of a particular make, or be fined. In 1578, the churchwardens received a fine of five shillings for this offence. During the sad period of the Great Plague, some other "items" read oddly enough now :—

" 1640. 'Item.' Paid to Eliz. James, she
  being *shut upp* 0 16 0
  For a truss of straw for her to lye on . 0 0 3
  For taking her to the hospital, where she
  died a pitiful creature . . . . 0 6 0"

In the bell room of the steeple is a record of the several peals that have been rung at various times. One is rather curious :—

" The College youths of this society did ring, on the 6th of October, 1776, a complete peal of 5040 Oxford treble bob-ten-in, in three hours and 45 minutes, with the sixth at home, twelve times wrong, and twelve times right, being the first performed here."

Bell-ringing, although noisy, is cheerful. It is said that England is the only country where the practice is reduced to a science, not beneath the notice of our best musical composers.

The church has some good monuments. The

most ancient one now left is one of a Lady Legh.
It is about twelve feet high.   Under an arch is the
effigy of Lady Legh, with an infant in her arms, and
one by her side.   She is depicted in the full dress of
the times, with her hair disposed in a number of
small curls.   The whole is carefully executed, and
the monument is a handsome one.

It bears the date of 1603.   This church had once
a good many old monuments, but during the usurpation of Cromwell many of them were destroyed, with
several fine brasses.   Near the altar, which is plain,
is a monument to a once celebrated person, Sir
Nicholas Butts, a learned scholar, and chief physician to Henry VIII.   There is an elegant monument in coloured marbles to the memory of Bishop
Gibson, who died in 1748.   There are several memorials to other bishops.   There are two very
handsome, stately monuments that may not pass
unnoticed.   One of them is a large slab of black
marble, supported by a white marble pedestal.   On
it stands a statue (almost too large for life) of
Viscount Mordaunt, in a roman habit, his coronet
and gauntlets being placed on elegant black marble
stands, at each side of the monument; while against
the wall are oval tablets recording his birth, death,
life and services.   The whole is beautifully done,
and does credit to the sculptors—for there were
two, Bushnell and Bird, who were, according to
Bowack, celebrated at that time.   It cost, according
to the same authority, £ 400.

Viscount Mordaunt is highly commended in Cla-
rendon's "History of the Rebellion."   A younger

son of the Earl of Peterborough, he commenced his remarkable career at an early age as a staunch Royalist, casting his lot with the King's fortunes. He partook of all the varied misfortunes, difficulties, and dangers of that exciting time, and played his part as an actor of no mean ability, and with spirit and energy. Upon the restoration of Charles II., that monarch loaded him with benefits. He was created Viscount Mordaunt, Lord Lieutenant of the County of Surrey, and Constable of Windsor Tower. He eventually died at Parson's Green, and was buried in this church.

The other handsome monument is to the memory of Lady Dorothy Clarke. The monument is stately, of white marble, fenced by iron rails. At the top is an urn, with beautiful festoons of flowers, supported by two winged genii, the work of that prince of flower sculptors, Grinling Gibbons. It cost £300., and is dated 1682. There is a pretty little monument to a Mrs. Catherine Hart. She is depicted with her four children in stiff dresses, all kneeling bolt upright, and all extremely well executed. At the bottom it is recorded that she " *lived virtuoslye and died godlie ye* 23 *daie of Octo.* 1605."

These are by no means all of the pretty tablets and small monuments in the church, erected, some to names well known to history, and others to wealthy and respectable inhabitants; but enough has been written to show that a visit to this interesting place would not be in vain to those who take interest in these things.

No less than eight bishops were buried in the

churchyard. Theodore Hook lived for some years in Fulham, at Egmont Villas, now pulled down to enable the Chelsea Waterworks Company to erect a bridge over the Thames to carry the water to London, and they wanted the ground on which the villa stood to erect a tower upon. Theodore Hook was buried in the churchyard opposite the chancel window. A stone marks his grave, with only the plainest of inscriptions. The churchyard, indeed, is full of good monuments, interspersed with trees, and it is altogether an interesting, beautiful churchyard.

CHAPTER III.

FULHAM PALACE, the residence of the Bishops of London, is very pleasantly situated on the banks of the Thames, and adjoins the Church. Its grounds, which are handsomely and romantically laid out, are nearly forty acres in extent —the whole is surrounded by a moat with two bridges. The broad bank that confines the moat forms a delightful promenade.

Part of the bank runs sideways with the Thames, so that on one hand the beautiful grounds of the palace are seen, and on the other charming views over the Thames. The Palace is ancient, and has always served as a residence for the Bishops of London. The greater part of it was built by Bishop Fitzjames in the reign of Henry VII., and was much larger than it is now, although at the present time it contains upwards of sixty rooms. In the year 1715 parts of it became ruinous. Sir Christopher Wren, and Sir John Vanbrugh examining it, it was decided to pull down a large portion, leaving it as it now stands. It is a venerable looking large plain building, in no way remarkable for ornamentation, or any particular style of architecture.

It is formed of brick and has two Courts. The

principal entrance is through an arched gateway into the great quadrangle, from which is the entrance into a noble hall fifty feet long, and twenty-seven wide; this fine room has been renovated from time to time, and over the chimney place are the arms of one of the bishops, Bishop Sherlock, they are handsomely carved in wood.

Hanging on the walls are also some fine full-length paintings of Henry VII., Queen Anne, and Queen Mary, with George II. In the lobby adjoining are some handsome oil paintings on paper, affixed to canvas, of Henry VIII., Thomas a Becket, and Margaret of Anjou.

There are many fine rooms in the Palace, among others, the dining room and the library. The contents of the latter were given by Bishop Porteous. The books are chiefly on theological and abstruse subjects. These two rooms open on the gardens. The library also is hung with well painted portraits of the Bishops of London, a good many of which are copies. There is a small neat chapel built by the present Archbishop of Canterbury when Bishop of London.

FULHAM PALACE GARDENS have been little altered since Bishop Grindall had them laid out. Bishop Compton greatly improved them. The gardens were once very celebrated. To them were brought many rare and beautiful trees and plants, and here was grown the first tamarisk tree seen in England. The gardens have a number of fine trees still standing; especially two monstrous ones—a hicory or American walnut tree, and a cedar of Lebanon, the largest it is said in England.

At the time when these beautiful productions of foreign lands were introduced, the gardens attracted more attention than they are likely to obtain in future, interesting as they are, from the reminiscences of the learned men who once walked among them.

Having two Horticultural and Botanical Gardens in London, with those of Kew and the Crystal Palace, nearly all the plants, flowers, and trees of other countries are familiar to us.

The most ancient, if not the most interesting relic connected with the Palace is the moat that runs entirely around it. It is both wide and deep, and is conjectured, not without good reasons, to be a work of the Danes, who visited Fulham in the autumn of 879, and encamped here for that winter; and as they generally stayed near the water and their ships, it is supposed that their camp occupied the spot where the Bishop's Palace now stands. None but a large body of vigorous men could have made such a long, deep and wide excavation. It is nearly a mile in its circuit, and is a great ornament to this part of Fulham.

The old, oddly built, quaint WOODEN BRIDGE, conducting from Fulham Church to Putney Church, is a very picturesque object. The views from the centre are very soft and pleasing. It was built about 1725, in a curious zig-zag style. It has been often anathematized in very strong language by the owners of steam boats and barges; for, indeed, what with its narrow arches or locks, and the sandbank in the river, navigation is dangerous and difficult. It is much valued by the inhabitants of the neighbourhood, who have hitherto stoutly and successfully resisted any effort to remove it.

The palace, the moat, the two churches, with the quaint bridge between them, and the softly flowing stream, form a group of interesting picturesque objects not often seen in one place. The Bishops of London and their servants, or any one in their employ, pass toll-free over this bridge as often as they please. This privilege was accorded to them in lieu of the ferry, which was in use before the bridge was built, and which belonged to them.

The Palace has been rendered for ever memorable and interesting by the residences of so many remarkable Prelates of various and widely differing characters, some of whom have left their memories to all time. Erkenwold was the fourth, and first remarkable, Bishop of London. To him was granted the Manor of Fulham. Of liberal notions, he laid out large sums of money on ecclesiastical purposes, and obtained by his vigour and perseverance many privileges for the clergy.

Bishop Bonner, one of the chaplains to Henry VIII, experienced a variety of fortunes not always of a dignified nature, and always using his abilities and power either openly or disguised to obstruct the Reformation. A favourite of Henry, and possessing considerable talent as a negotiator, he was employed to break off the marriage with Katherine, and also sent as Ambassador to Denmark, France, and Germany. Eventually he was made Bishop of London. In Edward the Sixth's reign he got imprisoned for

not enforcing some laws respecting the Reformation.
At liberty again in Mary's reign, he was included in
all the commissions for the trial and prosecution of
Protestants. As it was quite safe to do so, he had
by this time exhibited his character in its true light
as a cruel, bigoted Roman Catholic.

History records his cruelty during his seasons of
prosperity. Even at the Palace many brutal scenes
were enacted which he sanctioned, not only with his
presence, but actually perpetrated with his own
hand. It was in the beautiful gardens of his residence that on one occasion he had one Thomas Hen-
shaw fastened to a bench and most cruelly scourged
him with a rod. John Willes was punished in the
same way, after being kept eight days in the stocks.
The most sickening instance of his barbarity, however, was that of Tomkins a weaver. Though illite-
rate and of humble station, he was illustrious by his
fortitude, faith and exemplary piety, and sanctified by
his sufferings. Bonner examined him harshly in the
presence of the Archbishop and other noble persons.
Finding he could not make him recant, he then took
his hand and held it over a candle of three or four
wicks until the sinews actually shrank, and the flesh
was black.

For three years at that period he exercised his
cruel disposition. Hume computes that no less than
two hundred and thirty-seven men, women, and
children were tortured, burnt, or ruined by fines and
confiscations under his rule. Refusing to take the
oaths when Elizabeth came to the throne, he was
again imprisoned, and this time for life; for he died

in the Marshalsea; and was ignominiously buried at night.

History records no stronger contrast than the one afforded by his successor, Bishop Ridley; who, leading a holy life of blameless, gentle purity, was one of the brightest, as he was one of most efficient of the Protestant martyrs. As Bonner degraded, so Ridley hallowed the Palace by his residence. There are few biographies more quaint, .graphic, and deeply interesting than that of Fuller's account of this excellent prelate. His character, life, and horrible death, cannot be dwelt upon without exciting feelings of the highest admiration, and of the deepest commiseration.

Bishop Grindall was a remarkable and able prelate. He had been chaplain to Ridley, with whom he was deservedly a favourite. He assisted Ridley in compiling the Liturgy, and at his death succeeded to the bishopric. During his residence he laid out the gardens, and bestowed such care on his greenhouse, and his grapes were so highly celebrated, that every year Queen Elizabeth was presented with some. He afterwards became Archbishop of Canterbury, and died blind at Croydon.

The Bishops Sandys and Aylmer were both zealous Protestants, and the last conspicuous for humanity and kindness. Another of the bishops must not be passed over : Bishop Laud also passed the greater portion of his life at Fulham. Bishop Compton was also a prelate eminent alike for his scholastic attainments and abilities. He was the preceptor of the Princesses Anne and Mary, daughters of James II. In after years he assisted at their marriages : and later still he welcomed them back to this country.

Bishop Compton had a fine taste in gardening, and enriched and beautified the grounds of the Palace by bringing a large quantity of shrubs, trees, and plants, all at that time very rare, and some quite new to this country. For many years after his death these gardens were very highly and deservedly estimated.

He was a man of unbounded liberality and bene-volence, and led a life of strict piety and charity. He lived to the age of eighty-one years. There were many other bishops whose names deserve honourable and kindly notice, but their lives and characters are described in other works with so much more ability and learning than these pages pretend to exhibit; that the writer (although reluctantly) leaves them.

The first recorded public event that happened in Fulham was an incursion of the Danes in 879. They remained the winter, and appear to have done nothing more than dig the moat, described a few pages back. It is supposed they found Fulham not quite so defenceless as other places. During the civil war it was made the stage where the Royalists and Roundheads alternately enacted the strange and painful dramas of those times. The Puritans insulting and defacing the two churches of Putney and Fulham by breaking windows, destroying monu-ments, stealing the brasses, and even stabling their horses in the interior.

H

Fulham and its neighbourhood were indeed in a sore strait when Cromwell and his ironsides occupied it. Puritans quartered in every household. The whole place under the sternest discipline. The Vicar driven away, the Bishop deprived, and the Palace sold to a rough soldier; the wealthier inhabitants chased for their lives, and their goods appropriated.

This appears to have been the last public event that troubled the little Town.

CHAPTER IV.

LMOST every old large house in these four Parishes have a history attached to them. They were the homes, during their day, of celebrated historical characters : wits, beaus, beauties and scholars, who here played out their parts: unconscious of the interest and amusement posterity would take in their sayings and doings.

People certainly exhibited their characters more heartily and openly in those days than they do now, and seemed to be more in earnest than we are. For although we have doubtless the same variety of characters amongst us, yet the surface of society is rendered so smooth by the excessive refinement and high breeding considered indispensable among certain classes; and every kind of demonstrativeness is considered such an infringement of good taste, that the members of what is known as "good society" may be said to exhibit no character at all, being stereotyped editions of one another.

Fulham has more old houses still standing than the other parishes; but the majority of them do, indeed, present a melancholy appearance, having placards of "To let" on their venerable fronts.— Their wealthy inhabitants are deserting them; the numerous railways affording such facilities for travelling. They can live in more picturesque and bracing places, and actually reach them more easily.

A number of fine old mansions are standing on PARSON's GREEN, about half a mile from Fulham. It was once a pretty village, with the Parson's house (still standing) at the corner. The Green is left in the same state as when the parson and his family, and at other times the villagers, disported themselves upon it.

Large houses were built around it for the nobility and gentry, who had here their country seats. Of these the most remarkable is Peterborough House, which stands in large grounds, with a high wall all round it. It occupies the site of an old house known as " BRIGHTWELL's," in the reign of Elizabeth. The present mansion was rebuilt by Thomas Carey, son of the Duke of Monmouth. Two of its ancient gateways are still preserved ; they are of stone, curiously carved. One of them disguises the entrance to a stable, and the other forms part of an arbour. These gardens exhibited, about a hundred years ago, a remarkable tulip-tree, one hundred years old, and seventy-six feet high, bearing a large yellow tulip-shaped flower. It was said to be the first and last of its kind in this country.

PETERBOROUGH HOUSE has had some celebrated inhabitants. It was the property of that Lord Mordaunt, whose tomb in Fulham Church has been described, and his character, life, and services to his king and country briefly noticed. Here he lived and died. From him the estate descended to that extraordinary character, the celebrated Lord Peterborough, who married Anastatia Robinson, the well known singer.

His great abilities as a soldier and commander, as a councillor and orator, are evidenced by the various and numerous commissions of high trust and responsibility that were held by him ; and notwithstanding the multitude of occupations thus imposed upon him, he found time to cultivate the muses. Graceful and elegant in manners and person, he associated with all the wits and learned persons of his day. Pope, Swift, Locke, Gay, besides a host of others, were constant visitors at Parson's Green, for he exercised unbounded hospitality. His marriage was the oddest thing done by this universal genius.

Miss Anastatia Robinson, having for a long time resisted all improper offers of his, he at length married her in 1723, and took a house for her and her mother at Parson's Green, where she was visited by persons of high rank and respectability, who doubtless had the best of reasons to believe her to be his wife, or they would hardly have countenanced her and her mother. His lordship eventually, about twelve years afterwards, acknowledged his marriage at the Bath rooms, by desiring a servant to enter, and in a loud voice to announce that " Lady Peterborough's carriage waits."

The celebrated Sir Thomas Bodley resided at Parson's Green. He founded the Bodleian Library at Oxford, the contents of which are now more curious than useful perhaps; as by far the larger portion is on such abstruse subjects, that only very learned scholars are likely to use them.

Ivy Cottage, a long, low, picturesque house, covered with an aged ivy, was the residence of Oliver Cromwell, when he inflicted his visits on Fulham. It is still standing very near the Green.

A fine imposing old mansion, still standing in this place, and now empty, was formerly the residence of Samuel Richardson, the celebrated novelist, whose lengthy productions were read with such delectation by our predecessors.

Foote the dramatist resided at a favourite villa at Walham Green, then a pretty little village. It is now covered over by a multitude of very dirty little streets, with here and there a good shop, and a very fine church in the middle, built in the Gothic style, and dedicated to St. John. There are also some neat, pretty almshouses—"The Butchers' Almshouses"—and some flourishing National Schools, besides a large cocoa-nut fibre manufactory. But all this is modern. When Foote lived there, it was a pretty, secluded place. There are still standing several fine old trees, which appear to look with disgust on their present surroundings.

All the gay, the lively, and the fashionable of his time of course visited this celebrated dramatist. His abilities as an author and an actor, with his remarkably pleasing companionable qualities; his comic humour and talents as a mimic, made him the ornament of his age. When he died, some wit wrote :—

> "Foote from his earthly stage, alas ! is hurled,
> Death took him off, who took off half the world."

Normond House is another ancient house, used now as an asylum for ladies.

ELM PARK, the residence of Sir John Henniker, but who resides chiefly at Compton Manor in Somersetshire, is one of the finest and most interesting of the old mansions in the four parishes. It properly belongs to Chelsea; but as the entrance to it is in the Fulham Road an account of it is given here. Elm Park and house occupies a large portion of land known in old deeds as the "Sand Hills," later down as Chelsea Park; and it was then part of the estates of Sir Thomas More. Originally it was open fields. In 1625, however, a brick wall was built around it by the Lord Treasurer, Lord Cranfield. But greater part of the wall, if not all, has been taken down, and part of the land been built on. The park originally consisted of thirty-two acres.

At one time this land was planted with mulberry trees, with the intention of breeding the silk-worm: a patent was even obtained for the manufactory of raw silk. The public were much interested in it, and every effort made for its success, but in vain; for the variable temperature of England destroys the silk-worm. The next attempt to put the land to some use was an interesting and rather remarkable one. A Frenchman of some ability, Christopher Le Blon, built houses and erected looms for tapestry, with the design of copying Raphael's Cartoons. He made some very beautiful drawings for this purpose. The project was opened, and for a short time carried on by subscription. But it failed: several persons lost their money, and Le Blon disappeared. The mulberry ground, the houses and looms were all done away with, and a short time

afterwards the grand mansion now known as Elm
Park was built. It presents, grounds and all, an
exact specimen of an aristocratic house of the "olden
time." In most of the old houses standing about
these parishes some attempts have been made to
give them or their gardens a modern appearance;
but with good, and indeed rare taste, this fine old
place has been kept intact. To walk through its
stately rooms and about its old grounds is to step
back at once from modern life at least a hundred
and fifty years. There is a tradition that one of
Charles the Second's numerous mistresses resided
there, so a suspicion of royalty clings to the place.

A rather remarkable gentleman resided there for
some years, Sir Henry Wright Wilson. He married a daughter of the Earl of Aylesbury, and a very
odd circumstance happened to this lady. She went
frequently to the opera, and when there observed a
gentleman who did little else but stare at her, which
annoyed her greatly. One morning at breakfast she
was informed that an unknown individual of the
name of Wright had died at a mean lodging, and
left her an estate producing £3,000 a-year. Know-
ing no one of the name, she remembered how she
was persecuted by a pair of eyes at the opera; she
went to see him in his coffin, and recognized him.
In life they had never spoken to each other, and she
did not even know his name; nor could it have been
her beauty that attracted him, for she was very
plain. Sir Henry shortly afterwards lost this estate
for the expenses of contesting his seat as a member
of Parliament.

Sir Henry and his lady lived in great style, and in a free and generous manner. He was a magistrate, and in one of the large rooms in the house he held his Sittings; it is now locked up. An anecdote of the humorous way in which he sometimes shewed his displeasure is amusing. He had a very large establishment of well fed, well paid servants, whom prosperity, we suppose, had rendered a little insolent. Sir Henry had desired a carpenter, who was occasionally employed, to get a certain amount of work done in a given time. The carpenter required a little help, which the servants thought themselves above giving him. The work, therefore, was not done.

Sir Henry having been told the reason, said nothing until the next morning, when he ordered his carriage to be got ready with four horses, and astonished the servants by desiring the carpenter to seat himself in it. He himself accompanied it on horseback, and led the way through all the miry places he could find in the neighbourhood. Taking into consideration the state of the roads at that time, the condition of the carriage and horses may be perhaps imagined by the time he got back to Chelsea. He then desired the servants to clean the carriage and horses immediately or quit the house. He was a kind good master and they obeyed him. They never again, however, gave that carpenter any cause of complaint.

The exterior and interior of this fine old house gives ample evidence of the wealth and state in which its various tenants here lived. It is, or was,

a part of the Earl of Cadogan's estate. It contains
at least forty rooms, some of them very large and
handsome. The dining room is a fine specimen of
bygone taste and wealth. The ceiling and sides of
the room and mantelpiece are all richly decorated
with carving and devices that look like Grinling
Gibbons's work. It is the only room so profusely
ornamented, although nearly all the rooms are handsome. The grounds have been left in the old-
fashioned way they were laid out in. Some very
fine large elms are standing near the back of the
house, which may have given it the present name of
Elm Park.

Even the greenhouse gives one no idea of a
greenhouse of the present time. It looks like a
comfortable cottage with very large windows. High
walls shelter it from the Fulham Road.

The last old house to be noticed is a very interesting one, for it was the seat of " Nell Gwynne.'
It has been taken care of and well preserved by
various respectable families, who from time to time
have lived in it. It is a large white, plain, but
handsome house. The interior is of polished oak,
dark with age, but rich and handsome throughout.
Long, low, very comfortable rooms. The windows
once overlooked a park, which has been gradually
curtailed until only a moderate-sized garden back and
front is left. It stands a short distance from the
Thames. It now belongs to the Imperial Gas Company, who let it, and it is surrounded by their
works. There were four magnificent walnut trees,
planted by Royal hands. These have been cut

down ; for gas companies are very prosaic and practical in their operations : and as the trees were in the way, no considerations of their beauty or the interest attached to them prevented their destruction.

Numbers of persons go to see the old home of " poor Nell," whose errors as being a King's mistress have been so readily condoned by posterity, on account of her amiable, generous character, and that benevolence which was the origin of so noble an institution as the Chelsea Hospital.

Fulham boasts of a valuable manufactory, known as the WHITE GORGES PORCELAIN POTTERY. It is of ancient date, established so far back as 1684, by John Dwight, Esq., an Oxfordshire gentleman of fortune. He had been secretary to two successive Bishops of Chester. A patent was granted to him the same year.

Very beautiful dinner services, statuettes, figures, and jars were produced by this manufactory; as also transparent porcelain articles ; likewise a dark opaceous, red-coloured porcelain, known as China and Persian wares.

The old house in which the original proprietor lived still stands in the middle of the main street, still looking solemnly down on the little town, which has seen but few changes. The chief articles now produced are stone jars of a superior sort, and pots and other small things. Besides this, and the cocoanut manufactory at Walham Green, there are only the ordinary and necessary trades and small manufactories, most of them connected with gardening, carried on at this place.

There are a good many local charities and gifts to

the poor, arising from lands and monies bequeathed by pious donors of former ages, both to this parish and that of Hammersmith.

One of the most important of them is SIR WILLIAM POWELL'S ALMSHOUSES, founded in 1680, for poor men and women. These have recently (as they were very ugly and dilapidated) been pulled down and re-erected. They stand now adjoining the churchyard, and exactly opposite the vicarage, and have been built in good taste neatly and prettily in the Gothic style, with a long strip of well kept-grass plat before them. They are, however, not in keeping with the church or vicarage, forming a striking contrast to the last, which is a sedate, venerable, but very plain edifice. Fulham supports a large national school for three hundred children. An infant school and a new national school for boys were erected by voluntary contributions in 1860. All these schools are well maintained and conducted.

The late Right Honourable Laurence Sullivan, of Broome House, near the bridge, erected and endowed some useful, well managed schools, called the Elizabethan Schools, in Broomhouse Lane.

NORTH END is a suburb of Fulham. There is little to notice in the place, although it has been made into an ecclesiastical district, with a church, minister, and schools of its own. It has a population of 4,000, and is under the same social government as Fulham. There are several interesting old houses standing here and there, forming a not unpleasing contrast to the modern smart villas and good new houses that have been erected. There are four lunatic asylums in this parish.

HISTORICAL NOTICES.

—

Parish of Hammersmith.

HAMMERSMITH CHURCH.

Parish of Hammersmith.

CHAPTER I.

HAMMERSMITH, once the prettiest of hamlets, is now one of the largest and most flourishing of the suburbs of London. It is pleasantly placed on the left, or north bank of the Thames, and lies on the London clay. The air is peculiarly mild and soft; and it is well sheltered from cold winds by Hampstead and Highgate hills on the north, while on the south the Surrey hills protect it. It is not invigorating, but extremely well suited for the alleviation of bronchial and pulmonary complaints, and when offering retired walks and pretty scenery, was much resorted to by invalids suffering from these affections. It appears to derive its name from the Saxon word *Ham*, signifying a town, or collections of dwelling-places, and *Hyde*, or *Hythe*, a harbour, or creek, large enough to form a quay or dock for landing any kind of merchandize.

Numerous places on the banks of the Thames have names ending in Hythe,—such as Erythe, Greenhithe, now Greenwich, Queenhithe, Lambithe, now Lambeth, Chelsithe, now Chelsea, and other places.

There is no reliable data to be found for its present name " Hammersmith;" but in the court rolls of the early part of Henry VII.'s reign it was so called. Bowack has given an amusing but absurd legend for its designation: The two churches of Fulham and Putney being exactly alike, and exactly opposite to each other, with the river flowing between, were feigned to have been built by two pious sisters of gigantic stature, who had but one hammer between them, which, in throwing it across the water to each other, got broken. A smith residing at *Ham-hythe* mended it, enabling them to continue their pious employment; and the place afterwards was called *Hammersmith*. No doubt the fact of two pious sisters originally founding these two churches, and the name getting corrupted, or altered—as names do from age to age—suggested this legend.

The Great Western Road runs right through the parish,—a road once so well frequented by pack-horses, waggons, horsemen, and noblemen's carriages, stage coaches (and, it may be added, Highwaymen), with all the traffic now conveyed by railway; and, at convenient distances, those dear old inns of the old coaching days, smoking steeds, and loving cups, where travellers were welcomed like an old friend, and the arrangements for the comfort of those who sought their hospitality, however well paid for, was never dear at the price. To think of their cosiness and comfort makes one shudder at the new-fangled refreshment rooms of the railway stations: smartly painted and gilded as they are, with the indifference of the attendants and the indigestible cosmestibles, which the traveller is hardly allowed time to eat.

One of the old Roman roads was discovered in the year 1834, and traced through a large portion of its course; and in digging to make a road now known as Gold Hawk Road, they came to the old Roman causeway, made in the usual manner of those famous road-makers. Various coins and small matters were picked up, some of which have been preserved.

Hammersmith is a very ancient parish, and was included in the manor of Fulham, and mentioned in Domesday-book; its lands being even then highly cultivated. A few ages later both Hammersmith and Fulham were famous for their flowers and vegetables, and, indeed, served as a great fruit and kitchen garden for the London market.

Hammersmith is a polling place and police court district; it is about four miles from Hyde Park Corner. It was made into a separate parish in 1834 by an Act of Parliament, and was constituted into a vicarage. Its population in 1861 was 24,413; its rateable value is £80,000.

As it is included in the district of the Metropolitan Board of Works, it partakes largely of all the modern sanitary arrangements,—draining, paving, and abatement of nuisances. The effective and extensive drainage has cleared the air from the

I

aqueous particles with which it was once loaded; it
bids fair, therefore, to become one of the healthiest
of London suburbs.

It is not and never was, remarkable for its manufactures; but for Nurseries and Horticultural Gardens
it was once famous; it boasts of several even now
that it has been so built upon. The most remarkable
of these is LEE's NURSERY, known as the " Royal
Vineyard," situate near the high road, conducted now
by Mr. C. and Mr. Ed. Lee; it is an old establishment, carried on by three generations, ever since the
year 1760. Mr. James Lee, the original proprietor,
was a Scotchman. He entered into partnership with
a Mr. Kennedy, gardener to the then Lord Bolton,
and commenced business at the *Vineyard*, which,
about the middle of last century, was well known
as producing annually a considerable quantity of
Burgundy; the air and soil of Hammersmith being
favourable to the growth of the grape from which
this wine is made. But the increasing intercourse
with foreign countries caused this novel (at least in
England) branch of commerce to fail. In a house
which has been built in the grounds, lived for some
years, Worlidge, a celebrated engraver, who here
executed the most valuable of his productions. Mr.
James Lee and his partner took it and established a
most successful Horticultural Nursery, remarkable
for obtaining from distant countries everything rare
and beautiful to be obtained. They maintain a
collector at the Cape of Good Hope, and another
in America; so they are of world-wide celebrity.

Every known, rare, or new plant can be obtained there. They once received a letter addressed, "*Lee's Nursery, England*," which reached them readily. They were the first who brought *Tusia coccinea* to this country, and sold it for *a guinea* a plant. They also had the first China rose.

CHAPTER II.

HE SUSPENSION BRIDGE, the first of its kind hung over the river Thames, is a handsome ornament to Hammersmith. It was designed and built by W. T. Clark, Esq., engineer to the West Middlesex Water Works Company, who have very extensive works at this place. The foundation stone was laid by his Royal Higness the Duke of Sussex, on the 7th May, 1825, with considerable ceremony; winding up with a handsome dinner, without which, as is well known, no public ceremony whatever can be properly conducted.

Three hundred and fifty tons of iron were used to make this bridge. The suspension turrets are of stone : thirty six iron bars of various sizes sustain it. It has one hundred and thirty-five feet more of roadway than the Menai Bridge at Bangor in Wales. It cost £45,301. 10s. 9d.

The WEST MIDDLESEX WATER WORKS were established in this and the adjoining parishes in the beginning of the present century. The Grand Junction Canal is a great convenience to the place; it runs through the northern part of the parish, which is well supplied with railways, omnibuses, and all the modern appliances of Town.

Hammersmith, like its neighbour Chelsea, was formerly a highly aristocratic place, and although but few of the stirring events of history were enacted here, yet a great many celebrities of earlier times found here an agreeable dwelling place. The BROADWAY, with its green, now converted into roadway, and the houses around all used as shops, &c., was once daily thronged by the carriages of the gay and fashionable : many large noble mansions are yet standing which attest to the wealth and taste that erected them.

Decidedly the most interesting part of Hammersmith are the Malls, upper and lower, which, stretching along by the water-side, join CHISWICK MALL, also a handsome interesting place. Indeed the walk from the Suspension Bridge at Hammersmith to Kew Bridge is a very charming one; combining as it does memories of many high or famous personages; together with the noble river flowing so softly yet grandly by, and the number of large old beautiful trees which adorn the river side, and the grand old mansions ranged in such solemnity along. Some of these are standing back in their extensive old fashioned gardens, while the rest approach to within a short distance from the water, which is guarded here and there by brick copings, low enough to sit upon. The views from this place are very pretty, and have furnished "subjects" for the artist and a "theme" for poets, and the Suspension Bridge is seen to great advantage.

To give long biographical notices of the various celebrated or noble persons who about a hundred and fifty years ago had country residences here, would swell this work to proportions not intended by the writer; moreover, the dwelling places of a great many of them, like their inhabitants, are gone, pulled down; some built over with small cottages, others converted into places of business. However, a few of the persons who were remarkable in their day, will be alluded to : the curious in these matters are referred to Faulkner's works; and only those places which the writer has seen are mentioned in these pages.

UPPER AND LOWER MALLS are divided by a group of small mean tenements, known as LITTLE WAP-PING. The "Dove" coffee house has undergone but little alteration, and is well preserved. Thomson wrote his "Seasons" there in a room overlooking the river. Adjoining it is a four-roomed cottage known as the Duke of Sussex's smoking box. Opposite to it is the small mean house his Royal Highness dwelt in, when he resorted to Hammersmith for change of air. Charles II. resided for several years in a noble mansion in the Upper Mall; after his death his widowed Queen continued to live there, and built a capacious house known as the Banquetting House; it is even now very handsome, and attracts the attention of strangers. She also had the frontage of the Mall carried out in the form of a bastion, and planted elms which are now very large and handsome. Some of them, measured by the writer, are from fifteen to seventeen feet in girth. After her death, Dr. Radcliffe, an eminent physician, resided there. He was not only known for his abilities, but con-

spicuous for his drollery. Being penurious, he parted
with his money so unwillingly, that his tradesmen
found it a hard matter to get paid. One of them, a
persevering paviour, insisting on having his debt, he
said to him, " Why, you have only spoilt my pavement, and then covered it over with earth to hide
your bad work." " Doctor," said the paviour, " mine
is not the only bad work the earth hides." " Witty,
are you," said the Doctor, " why, you *must* be poor ;
come in and be paid."

Lord Allington, Sir George Warburton, and the
Duke of Norfolk afterwards successively resided
there. Eventually it got into the possession of
George the Fourth's head cook and purveyor, as well
as owner of the Pavilion at Brighton, Louis Weltjie,
Esq. Sir Godfrey Kneller also lived in the Mall.

HAMMERSMITH TERRACE is a sedate, solemn, respectable row of houses by the river side ; the back
of them is laid out prettily for a pleasure garden
in common. At number five lived and died Mrs.
Mountain the singer, whose sweet strains so often
charmed the ears of our fathers and grandfathers.

At number thirteen lived that extraordinary
painter, J. De Loutherburg. He came to England
at the request of Garrick to superintend the scenery
at Drury Lane Theatre, about 1770. He was an
excellent landscape painter, although a certain excessive richness of colouring he gave to his scenery is
offensive to severe critics, who characterise it as
gaudy and extravagant. He lived a respectable
moral life ; therefore the delusion he fell into respecting himself, and so cleverly impressed upon

others, (for great numbers believed in him) is not to
be accounted for.   He asserted boldly that he had
been gifted with miraculous powers of healing all
known complaints and disorders, by the *power of
sympathy;* he merely looked at his patients and they
were cured!   Some of his admirers published a long
list of cures, too long and too absurd to be noticed
gravely.   His fame was great and followers numerous.   He was buried in Chiswick churchyard, which
lies in such a sweet spot by the Thames which
flows so gently here.   A handsome tomb, with a
well written, long, but rather fulsome epitaph, was
erected to his memory.

Time, and the exigencies of modern civilization,
are destroying as fast as they can the substantial
mansions of the olden times, more especially in the
suburbs.   The last thirty or forty years has completely changed the face of the country within reach
of our insatiable Metropolis.   The old mansions are
gone, and their places occupied by cold, comfortless,
ugly erections of "Villas," "Lodges," &c., which
will never be *ancient.*   Surely nothing can be more
flimsy and fragile than the majority of the houses
built in these times.   To be sure they will not be
standing long enough to make the next generations
wonder at the want of taste and care so distressingly
displayed in them.   However, a great many grand
old dwellings are left here and there in these four
Parishes.

In addition to those in the Mall, an interesting
one, with two handsome cedars in its quaint old
garden, has been left close to the old church—

BRADMORE HOUSE; of which a long account is given in Faulkner.

BROOK GREEN, a very genteel part of Hammersmith, has several, especially one called THE EAGLES, built in the reign of Queen Anne. It is very large and handsome,—in an old-fashioned style, that is. Theresa Terrace is an old substantial terrace for the better classes, and will no doubt afford comfortable homes to many generations long after the majority of modern terraces have disappeared. St. Peter's Square, close to a plain, substantial church of that name, has comfortable genteel residences for those who can afford to live there.

Cedar trees must have been plentiful at Hammersmith, so many of them are still to be seen at either the back or front of the older houses.

Hammersmith is remarkable for its schools, owing we suppose to so many houses which are too large for persons of ordinary means to support, and standing generally in large gardens. Their internal arrangements, with the mild air, is suitable to educational establishments. The tide of fashion flowing now in other directions, the owners are glad to let them at a moderate rent.

CHAPTER III.

HE PARISH CHURCH was consecrated in 1631 by Bishop Laud. It was the last church he consecrated. It was originally a chapel of ease to Fulham Church, Hammersmith at that time being in the parish of Fulham; but since the division of the two parishes took place in 1834, it has been reckoned as the parish church. It is a plain, spacious, handsomely built brick structure. The altar piece is handsome, although very heavy; as it is of oak, or painted oak colour, from top to bottom, consisting of three stories of the Corinthian order, with slabs for seven large candlesticks, carved and gilt. The pilasters and compartments are ornamented with rich carvings of foliage and cherubs, supposed to be the work of Grinling Gibbons. The paintings on the walls and ceiling of the chancel represent adoring angels, with rich drapery, supported by cherubs. Cipriani, the celebrated artist who painted Brandenburgh House, was employed. There are some interesting monuments; one of the most noticeable is of handsome black marble, against the wall, to the memory of Alderman Smith. He is represented in the full official dress of an alderman of the sixteenth century, and is oddly enough supported by two weeping female figures.

Another adjoining, to the memory of Sir Edward Neville, is rather elegant. On the east wall of the north gallery is a handsome tablet of white and veined marble, in the form of a pyramid, commemorating the death of George Pring, Esq., the projector of Hammersmith Suspension Bridge. There is also a fine bronze bust of Charles I., erected by Sir Nicholas Crispe, whose heart was buried at the foot of the pedestal. He was a loyal subject of, and sufferer in the misfortunes of that unhappy monarch. Sir Nicholas Crispe was a munificent benefactor to the church of this, his native place; for he was born at Hammersmith. He was one of the most zealous, upright, brave and sensible friends and followers the King ever had. The old church door is approached by a handsome avenue of limes, trimmed and trained to a state of neatness. It has a quadrangular tower, supported by graduated buttresses. It has six good bells. The living is a vicarage in the gift of the Bishop of London.

There is yet another interesting reminiscence attached to the church. Queen Caroline (George the Fourth's consort) dwelt for some months at Brandenburgh House. On one occasion a curious and interesting procession left the East Gate of that place. The principal inhabitants, with all the parish functionaries appeared, each carrying a white wand, and conducted her, all on foot, to the Church, where she publicly received the Holy Sacrament from the hands of the Rev. Mr. Leggatt. Afterwards, special prayers were solemnly offered up for her welfare.

St. Peter's is a handsome stone church. St. John's is also a fine, well-built structure. Another handsome church is to be erected in a wretched neighbourhood near Kensington Railway Station. The foundation stone was laid by Lady Barrow on the 22nd of October, 1870. There are various dissenting chapels.

The most beautiful church in Hammersmith is the one at Shepherd's Bush.

SHEPHERD'S BUSH is a mile from Hammersmith, and three from the Marble Arch, London. Once a very small village, surrounded by wild waste lands, it is now a rapidly rising, smart London suburb. It is dry, airy, and very healthy, and bids fair to be respectably populated.

Near this place is WORMWOOD SCRUBS. It was once a large wild wood of two hundred acres. In 1812 Government took it on a long lease at £100. per annum. It has been levelled and properly prepared for the exercise of troops of soldiers, the various companies of volunteers, and others.

There is a very elegant church, built and endowed at the cost of the late Bishop Blomfield, dedicated to St. Stephen. It is built in the Decorated style, of stone, with a spire and tower rising to a height of 150 feet, and forms a graceful and conspicuous object from every point of approach. It is fitted with carved oaken benches, to hold six thousand persons. Three thousand of these seats are free ; its windows are filled with beautifully stained glass.

It cost £ 10,000., and was indeed a munificent gift. There are four services a day, and four sermons preached every Sunday.

All the churches have excellent schools attached to them, both national and infant, all well conducted and flourishing: and all have Sunday schools as well.

At the corner of Brook Green stands a Roman Catholic chapel and training college, with almshouses and school, the whole erected in the Gothic style, and forming handsome and striking objects.

The Roman Catholics have also a Reformatory for boys at Blythe House. Near the Broadway is a convent of English Benedictine nuns, founded 1669. There is also a convent of " Good Shepherds," in an old house formerly known as Beauchamp House. It is one of the most charitable institutions in the country. Women of lost reputation are here instructed in moral and religious training, and taught to earn their living in some honest way. There is a class of Magdalens for those who decline to enter the world again.

Besides these, there are classes for the preservation and detention of young children. There is also another convent, devoted partly to the aged, and partly to diseased crippled infants ; so these benevolent institutions embrace all classes and all ages. Hammersmith is rich in charities and schools, both old and new. Edward Latymer, in 1624, bequeathed thirty-five acres of land for the clothing of poor men and boys, and educating the latter.

The land now is so valuable that it provides for
thirty men, one hundred boys, and fifty girls.

The educational establishments of Hammersmith
have received a valuable addition in the new institution known as ST. GODOLPHIN SCHOOL; it is close to
St. John's Church.   It has playgrounds four acres
in extent.   The foundation stone was laid by the
Bishop of London in June, 1861.   It can accommodate two hundred boys.   There are class rooms,
dining hall, and dormitories for forty boarders, and
a handsome residence for the head master.   It is a
public Grammar School, founded in accordance with
the will of William Godolphin, Esq.   For a yearly
payment of eight pounds, boys in the neighbourhood
are instructed in all the acquirements of a liberal
education.   It has been so prosperous, that two
small branches have been opened at a little distance
in the town.

The town supports a well-written newspaper, *The
West London Observer*.   The West London Hospital is highly creditable to the inhabitants of Hammersmith; it is conducted on liberal principles, and
is open day and night to all cases and patients of all
denominations.

Fishing was once quite an institution at Hammersmith, and supported a number of families.
Some years ago, when the Thames was so plenti-
fully supplied with the fish usually obtained in fresh
waters, it was caught in considerable quantities, and
sent to the London market.   Naturally this trade
declined as the fish deserted the Thames.

The Mall, however, is very lively in the summer, when the row boats are in requisition for pleasure parties and all sorts of aquatic amusements. A large, handsome house of entertainment—the "Rutland Hotel"—has been built in the Mall, which is in no want of customers when the season commences.

CHAPTER IV.

THE very earliest historical event that happened in Hammersmith was the irruption of those pests of the early ages, the Danes, who ravaged and burnt with their usual ferocity.

In after ages, the quiet rural precincts of Hammersmith was made the stage upon which a portion of the scenes of the Civil War was enacted,—a war which spread ruin and desolation over the land, and equalled, if not exceeded, in cruelty anything done by the Danes. Hammersmith has always been noted for its loyalty; and one of the brightest ornaments of the Civil War was a native of Hammersmith, Sir Nicholas Crispe, whose loyalty to his King, Charles II., was only equalled by his attachment to the Established Church. He was in all respects a brilliant and remarkable character; uniting many rare and estimable gifts with the most practical common sense. Born heir to a large estate, and a gentleman by education and birth, he was so inoculated with a love of business that, amidst all the distractions of the Civil War, he contrived to carry on such extensive dealings in foreign lands, that it brought in £100,000. a-year to the exchequer.

All the correspondence and supplies of arms which

were obtained by the Queen in Holland, and by the King's agents in Denmark, were consigned to him, and by his prudence and vigilance found their way safely to the appointed places. His zeal and ardour were so great that, when wishing to conduct any particularly delicate and secret business, he trusted it to no one, but conducted it himself, nor cared what disguises he assumed. He often passed between Oxford and London as a butter-woman on horse-back, between a pair of panniers. Again, he would be at the water-side with a basket of flounders on his head, besides various other disguises; and he never failed to attain his ends. He was equally distinguished as a military commander. At his own expense he raised a regiment of horse for the King, put himself at its head, and performed many signal services. The King's affairs becoming desperate, he embarked with Lord Culpeper and Colonel Monk for France. Being eventually allowed, on certain conditions, to return to England, he turned his attention to business again, and continued to send the King assistance of monies.

Upon Cromwell's death, he was greatly instrumental in urging the citizens of London to give the proper amount of encouragement to General Monk. When Charles returned, he made him a Baronet, and reinstated him as Farmer of the Customs. Finally, he passed the last four years of his useful life at his native place, Hammersmith; and here he died. His body was interred in the vault with his ancestors, in St. Mildred's, Bread Street, London, while his loyal heart was buried beneath the bust of his loved master and king in Hammersmith Church. Sir Nicholas Crispe had built himself a noble house at Hammersmith, which, during his absence, Cromwell occasionally made his head-quarters, while General Fairfax and other officers were quartered at Butterworth (now pulled down and built on), belonging to Lord Mulgrave. While there, the officers amused themselves by breaking the windows and otherwise damaging the church, as their residence was near that sacred edifice. To this day the memory of Sir Nicholas Crispe is justly held in great estimation in Hammersmith.

There are several old inns left in this parish, but there is nothing noticeable in their appearance, and they have been so patched up and disguised, that if ever they were picturesque they have lost all pretensions to it now. There was one, which has not long been pulled down, that has been drawn by many artists, and that was indeed a quaint affair. Hammersmith has a neat Cemetery. A handsome well-built Union Workhouse serves for this place and Fulham : it is in the Fulham Road.

The New Road turning off to the right from the end of the town is a very pleasant part of Hammersmith. It is a long, wide, good road, with good residences at intervals interspersed with trees, and conducts to Shepherd's Bush. Very highly respectable families reside there, and it is altogether a pleasant place to live in, and forms a good clean walk in all weathers.

BISHOPS OF LONDON

FROM THE FOUNDATION OF THE SEE.

	A.D.		A.D.
Melitus	605	Alfstern	959
Ceadda	654	Wulfston	981
Wina	666	Alhunus (c)	1004
Erkenwald (a)	675	Alroy	1016
Waldonus	685	Elfward	1032
Ingualdas	715	Rob. Gemeticensis .	1044
Egnulphas	727	Guilielmus	1050
Wighed	756	Mauritius (d)	1087
Eadbright	761	Richard De Beaumes	1108
Eadgar	768	Gilbert	1128
Kenwalgus	773	Robert de Segillo (e)	1141
Eadbald	784	Richard Beaumes	1152
Heckbert	795	Gilbert Foliot	1163
Osmond	813	Richard Nigellus	1189
Ethelnob	835	Guilielmus de Sancta	
Ceolbert	838	Maria	1199
Ranulphus	841	Eustachius de Fau-	
Snithulfus	854	conbridge	1221
Eadstan	860	Roger Niger	1229
Wulfsius	873	Fulco Basset	1244
Ethelwerd	878	Henry de Wing-	
Elston	886	ham (f)	1259
Theodred	900	Richard Talbot	1262
Wulstan	922	Henry de Sandwich	1263
Brithelmus	941	John de Chishul	1274
Dunstan (b)	958	Richard de Gravesend	1280

A.D.		A.D.
Richard de Baldock	1304	Nicholas Ridley(*m*)	1550
Gilbert Seagrove ...	1313	Edmund Grindall (*n*)	1559
Richard Newport...	1317	Edmund Sands(*o*) .	1571
Stephen Gravesend	1318	John Aylmer ...	1576
Richard Bintworth .	1338	Richard Fletcher...	1594
Ralph Stratford ...	1339	Richard Bancroft .	1597
Michael Northbrook	1354	Richard Vaughan .	1604
Simon Sudbury (*g*)	1361	Thomas Boves ...	1607
William Courtney .	1375	George Abbott ...	1609
Robert Braybrook .	1381	John King... ...	1611
Roger Walden ...	1404	George Mountaigne	1621
Nicholas Bubworth	1406	William Laud (*p*) .	1626
Richard Clifford ...	1407	William Juxon ...	1633
John Kemp ...	1422	Gilbert Sheldon ...	1660
William Gray ...	1426	Humphrey Hinchan	1663
Robert Fitshugh ...	1431	Henry Compton (*q*)	1675
Robert Gilbert ...	1436	John Robinson ...	1713
Thomas Kemp ...	1449	Edward Gibson ...	1723
Richard Hill ...	1489	Thomas Sherlock ..	1748
Thomas Savage ...	1496	Thomas Hayter ...	1761
William Warham (*h*)	1502	Richard Osbaldeston	1762
William Barnes ...	1504	Richard Terrick ...	1764
Richard Fitsjames (*i*)	1506	Robert Lowth ...	1777
Cuthbert Tunstall (*k*)	1522	Beilby Porteus ...	1787
Edmund Bonner(*l*)	1540	John Randolph ...	1809

The present Bishopric of London is held by the Right Hon. and Right Rev. John Jackson, D.D., author of many able theological works, besides numerous tracts and pamphlets.

NOTES.

(*a*) Erkenwald. A bishop of very enlarged ideas and much learning; he was the son of Offa, king of the East Saxons. By his energy and liberality he obtained many privileges for the clergy.

(*b*) Bishop Dunstan was said to be a good musician, painter, and mechanic. He had been Abbot of Glastonbury and Worcester, then Bishop of London, and eventually Archbishop of Canterbury. He was remarkable for opposing the marriage of the clergy.

(*c*) Alhunus, tutor to Edmund Ironside and Edward the Confessor.

(*d*) Bishop Mauritius. He was chaplain to William the Conqueror, and afterwards Chancellor. He refounded and greatly contributed to the building of St. Paul's Cathedral, which had been destroyed by fire.

(*e*) Robert de Segillo was made bishop by Queen Matilda. In the wars of his reign he was made prisoner in his own palace, and regained his liberty by paying a heavy fine.

(*f*) Bishop Wingham was Lord High Chancellor in the reign of Henry III., who often visited him at the Palace.

(*g*) Bishop Sudbury became Archbishop of Canterbury 1375, and was beheaded in Wat Tyler's Rebellion in 1381.

(*h*) Bishop Warham, a prelate of great learning and ability as a lawyer, a statesman, and a divine. Living in the reign of Henry the Seventh, he was successively Master of the Rolls, Keeper of the Great Seal, and Lord High Chancellor, becoming Bishop of London in 1502, and eventually Archbishop of Canterbury.

(*i*) Bishop Fitsjames rebuilt the great quadrangle of the Palace.

(*k*) Bishop Tunstall, a prelate of high character, eminent for his abilities and goodness ; he was imprisoned several times, and eventually died a prisoner, in the reign of Elizabeth, as a Catholic refusing to take the oaths.

(*l, m*) Of these two bishops—Bonner and Ridley—the first died in prison for refusing to take the Protestant oaths, and Bishop Ridley was burnt for refusing to be a Catholic. The only redeeming point in Bishop Bonner's character is his firm adherence to his principles.

(*n*) Bishop Grindall, who improved the Palace Gardens, was a divine of remarkable ability. He assisted Fox in collecting information for his "Book of Martyrs," and also assisted Ridley in compiling the beautiful Liturgy used in the Church of England.

(*o*) Bishop Sands. Highly valued by Elizabeth; he was appointed to assist in the celebrated Conference held with the Roman Catholic divines, and also assisted in the new translation of the Bible in her reign.

(*p*) The celebrated Bishop Laud was born at Reading, and was the son of a clothier of that place. A learned scholar, but of bigoted views, he passed the earlier part of his public life in contentions with the Puritans, a sect which even then was gaining ground; he violently, and always so contemptuously, opposed their principles, that eventually, when they had the power, they destroyed him. In 1640 he was accused by Parliament of high treason, and sent to the Tower; after a trial of twenty days, he was beheaded in 1644 or 45. He was Archbishop of Canterbury; and the afternoon before he went to prison, he gathered all his household together in the fine old chapel of Lambeth Palace, and performed the Evening Service for the last time, reading some appropriate psalms, and taking leave of them in a beautiful prayer.

(*q*) Bishop Compton, one of the worthiest of divines. He took part in the troubles of those times, and was treated with much resentment by the Catholic party, at that time gaining ground under the Duke of York, who lived such a short reign as James II. He was sequestered in his palace at Fulham, and was suspended from his see. While under this cloud, he passed his time in beautifying and enriching the gardens. He had a fine taste, and also had a scientific knowledge of the subject; and for many years afterwards these gardens were remarkable for the beauty and value of the numerous trees and plants he had so tastefully disposed about the grounds.

RECTORS OF CHELSEA,

COMMENCING WITH THE FIRST ON RECORD.

	A.D.		A.D.
Roger de Berners	1316	Reginald Heber (a)	1766
Nicholas Horsbound	1339	Thomas Drake, D.D.	1770
Martyn de Moulish	1348	W. B. Cadogan ...	1775
William Palmer ...	1368	Charles Sturges ...	1797
Thomas de Preston	1369	Hon. and Rev. Dr.	
John Laske ...	1530	Wellesley (b) ...	1805
John Richardson ...	1543	Rev. Dr. Lockwood	
Richard Ward ...	1585	Charles Kingsley...	
Adam Littleton, D.D.	1669	G. A. Blunt ...	
John King, D.D. ...	1694	John Rush ...	
Sloane Elsmere, D.D.	1699		

The present Rector is the Rev. R. H. Davies, who succeeded in 1855.

(a) Father of the late lamented Reginald, Bishop of Calcutta.

(b) Was brother of the late Duke of Wellington.

VICARS OF KENSINGTON,

FROM THE FIRST ENDOWMENT OF THE VICARAGE.

	A.D.		A.D.
Bagot de Berthosp-		Robert Cade ...	
vol Westrop ...	1260	John Ifield ...	1465
Wm. de Northton .		Edmund Aspys ...	1484
Henry de Driffield	1322	John Sampson ...	1492
Thomas de Ryeleppe	1328	John Judson ...	
John Wyseman ...	1336	John Parsons ...	1519
John de Kernetby		John Batemanton...	1556
Gilbert Rawlein ...	1363	Geo. Leedes ...	1558
Wm. de Lydington	1370	Leonard Watson,	
John Thomas ...		M.A.	1563
John Trigg ...	1372	Henry Hopkins ...	1571
John Charleton ...	1373	Henry Withers, M.A.	1571
W. Gaston ...		Richard Elkins ...	1608
Phillip Montgomery	1388	Thomas Hodges,	
Richard Stokes ...	1391	M.A. (a) ...	1641
Roger Paternoster	1394	William Wigan ...	1672
Wm. Tonge ...	1395	John Millington ...	1700
Hame de la More .	1396	Robert Tyrwhitt ...	1728
John Smith ...	1400	John Wilcox ...	1731
John Wellys ...		John Jortin, D.D. .	1762
Rob. Caldicott ...	1415	James Waller, D.D.	1770
David Spark ...	1418	Richard Ormerod .	1795
Wm. Roper ...	1432	Thos. Rennell, M.A.	1816
Rich. Rumney ...	1443	R. Potts, M.A. ...	1822
Richard More ...	1451	The Venerable Arch-	
John Locke ...	1461	deacon Sinclair .	1842

(a) Rev. T. Hodges. He was a distant relative of that foppish Earl Holland, who went to the scaffold, when he was executed, in a white satin waistcoat, &c. The Rev. Mr. Hodges attended his lordship thither.

VICARS OF FULHAM.

Name	A.D.	Name	A.D.
Henry Martin	1329	James Aynsworth	1511
Thomas Offring	1361	Rob. Egremont	1513
John Goding	1392	Rob. Newton	1529
Gilbert Janyn		Joseph Smyth	1545
Walter Gerard	1397	Nicholas Smyth	1550
John Stevens	1416	William Hewett	
Richard Eaton		Christopher Goffe	1591
John Sudbury	1434	Andrew Smyth	1593
Henry Smith	1451	Peter Lily	1598
Wm. Layton	1452	Thomas Walkington	1615
Henry Watfree	1453	Richard Cluett (a)	
Wm. Redenes	1461	Adonirum Bryfield	1649
Richard Hendock	1463	Isaac Kright	1657
John Cooke	1465	Edward Kerne	1660
John Elton, B.D.	1466	Vincent Barry	1691
John Chadalworth	1467	Phillip Dwight, D.D.	1708
Wm. Lax		W. N. Blomberg	1733
Wm. Harvey		Samuel Knight	1750
John Petitot	1471	Denison Cumber-	
Walter Newton	1472	land (b)	1757
Richard Seffrey	1476	Anthony Hamilton	1763
John Cooper	1479	Graham Jepson, B.D.	1776
Wm. Stokes	1481	William Wood, B.D.	1811
John Woodhouse	1502	Rev. R. G. Baker,	
John Phipps	1503	M.A., Prebendary	
Adam Forster	1506	of St. Paul's	1820

(a) He was chaplain to the Bishop of Chichester, a justice of the peace, and at the Rebellion suffered greatly for his loyalty.

(b) Father of the celebrated Richard Cumberland.

CURATES OF HAMMERSMITH

UNTIL 1834, WHEN IT WAS MADE A VICARAGE.

	A.D.		A.D.
J. Dent	1631	F. Allen	1740
Isaac Kright ...	1647	T. Rayne	1751
Mathew Fowler, D.D.	1661	T. Sampson ...	1757
J. Wade	1662	Dr. Smith	1763
Michael Hutchinson, D.D. ...	1707	T. S. Atwood ...	1788

The present Vicar of Hammersmith is the Rev. James Connell, M.A., of King's College, Cambridge.

CONCLUSION.

THE writer of these pages has given but meagre statistics of the four parishes, for two reasons. As the four places are all in the London district, very ample particulars of these things may be so readily obtained at either of their Vestry Halls. Also, the particulars of the new Census will in a short time be made public. All the four parishes are busy in building and improving their respective districts. Of the four, however, Chelsea appears to be the most active in works of utility; and even amusements, as of late it even boasts of an elegant little theatre, opened in Sloane Square. So that, with Cremorne Gardens, it has two places of public entertainment, which are well supported considering how far they are from London. The other parishes make no attempts of this kind. At Fulham is a Working Man's Institute, and now and then a concert. Kensington and Hammersmith have only Penny Readings and occasionally concerts.

Chelsea and Kensington have each their own Workhouse. Fulham and Hammersmith a handsome well-built Union Workhouse for the two parishes. All the parishes support local news-

papers, which are really well written and supplied,
and at a very moderate charge. Of the cemeteries belonging to them, Kensington has decidedly
the largest and handsomest. The CEMETERY at
WEST BROMPTON is very elegantly laid out. It has
a noble avenue, bordered by a double row of fir
and lime trees, which are very effective. It is
crowded with very excellent, and some very beautiful, monuments, enclosing the remains of high and
celebrated persons; one of the most conspicuous
of the monuments is one raised by public subscription to the late Alfred Mellon, as some testimony to his musical abilities and as a well-merited
tribute to his character. Around his tomb lie many
Actors and Actresses of note. This cemetery is
well worthy of a visit, and in the summer it is
much resorted to. The flowers and trees so profusely adorning it, rob it of the melancholy usually
attendant on these places : the other cemeteries
are also very pretty and neat.

With the exception of Fulham, all the four
parishes are amply supplied with every kind of conveyance by means of cabs, omnibuses, and railways,
a conveyance of some kind or other leaving the
last three parishes every five minutes or so. The
postal arrangements are the same as in London.

THE END.

DRYDEN PRESS: J. Davy & Sons, 137, Long Acre, London.

www.ingramcontent.com/pod-product-compliance
Lightning Source LLC
Chambersburg PA
CBHW020556270326
41927CB00006B/864